How to Make Your
Sales Presentations $ing!

ANNE MILLER

AMACOM
American Management Association

New York • Atlanta • Boston • Chicago • Kansas City • San Francisco • Washington, D.C.
Brussels • Mexico City • Tokyo • Toronto

This publication is designed to provide accurate and authoritative
information in regard to the subject matter covered. It is sold with the
understanding that the publisher is not engaged in rendering legal,
accounting, or other professional service. If legal advice or other expert
assistance is required, the services of a competent professional person
should be sought.

Library of Congress Cataloging-in-Publication Data

Miller, Anne.
    Presentation jazz / Anne Miller.
       p.   cm.
    Includes bibliographical references and index.
    ISBN 0-8144-7962-6
    1. Sales presentations.   I. Title.
    HF5438.8.P74M55   1998
    658.85—dc21   98–18410
                                            CIP

Printing number

10 9 8 7 6 5 4 3 2 1

In memory of my father,
Leon Miller

Contents

Acknowledgments

First and foremost, I want to thank Janine Gordon, President of Emmerling Post Gordon Public Relations in New York City. Her boundless enthusiasm, generosity, and faith were directly responsible for my completing this book. Everyone should have a cheerleader like Janine in their lives!

Gratitude also goes to Jim Donoghue, Jim Fishman, Marcia Grace, Marilyn Thypin, Steve Rivkin, and my brother Jay for their early comments, suggestions, and direction. Katerina Catersano, President of Network Design and Communications, has my eternal admiration and respect for her professionalism and patience in putting the manuscript together. Thanks also to Jeff Herman, my agent, who saw the potential in this new approach to creating winning presentations, and then, to Jacquie Flynn, Ellen Kadin, and Mike Sivilli, my editors, for helping me successfully translate my ideas into book form.

And to the thousands of executives and salespeople who have either participated in my seminars, heard me at a conference, or had private coaching, my deep appreciation for the privilege of working with you and for teaching me so much about the "music" of winning sales presentations.

Introduction

Jazz! Up Your Presentations

Jazz is music that *moves* people—to nod their heads and tap their feet. *Sales music* is a presentation the *moves* prospects—to make a commitment and say yes! Presentation Jazz! is a framework that shows you how to be a virtuoso sales musician: a person who makes winning presentations on a consistent basis easily and without stress.

The Challenge

Getting that yes from buyers to your sales message in today's business environment has become increasingly difficult for salespeople everywhere. Buyers are busier than ever. They are very sophisticated and demanding. As products and services become more alike within their competitive fields, it is harder and harder for buyers to see differences in value among them. In many fields, salespeople are encountering new, unexpected competitors. For example, newspaper, magazine, and network television advertising salespeople who are accustomed to competing only with one another for a client's advertising dollars now find themselves having to compete with cable television and the Internet for the same budgets.

These external pressures from buyers are compounded by internal pressures to close business from sales managers, who themselves are under pressure to meet aggressive corporate revenue and profit goals.

The poor salesperson is caught in the middle. What was once a simpler "pat-'em-on-the-back, take-'em-to-lunch" relationship sales job has become a complex, strategic battle to win business. For all these reasons, getting your message across to customers is a challenging, difficult job.

The Solution Evolves

In my seminars, I saw salespeople increasingly weighed down by these business changes. This was across the board in industries ranging from publishing to telecommunications. While working through various sales presentation problems with workshop attendees, I would often find myself using music metaphors to explain key points about the nature of winning sales presentations. I would talk about the "music" of a successful sales presentation, how the elements in it had to flow, move, and catch buyers, how there was a rhythm to a strong sales message, and how star sales presenters, intuitively or otherwise, integrated all these elements into a winning story.

Eventually, I realized that the music metaphor could be used in a very deliberate way to help sales representatives develop winning presentations on a consistent basis. I refined and tested that concept with hundreds of salespeople over a period of years, and that's how the general idea for the music metaphor, which is the theme of this book, was developed.

If music is the running metaphor, why is jazz the particular type of music chosen? As I was thinking about the music-presentation connection, I was also going to various jazz clubs in New York. I noticed that when people listened to jazz, they were caught up in the music in a subtle way. Almost involuntarily, they started to move as they became involved. They tapped their feet or fingers, or they nodded their heads to the beat. That happens when listening to other types of music as well, but the unique thing about the jazz audiences I saw was the close attention they paid to everything they were hearing. It struck me that that's what happens to buyers when a presentation is working properly.

Buyers get caught up in the seller's story and they also start to move. They lean forward with real interest to hear what the seller has to say. They often nod silently in agreement with the selling points. They ask questions. They pay close attention to what the seller is showing them. They pick up a pen to take notes. And, ultimately, they are *moved* to say yes!

I combined the winning-presentation-as-sales-music metaphor with the reactions people have when they listen to jazz into an easy-to-use framework, or model, and the result is *Presentation Jazz! How to Make Your Sales Presentations $ing!*

How Does It Work?

The Jazz! framework works for you in two ways. First, prior to giving a presentation, it is a *structuring tool* to help you organize your thoughts, facts, data, and ideas quickly and easily into the most powerful selling message possible. Second, Jazz! can be used as an *assessment tool* to measure the selling power of your presentation. It enables you to review a completed presentation to correct any relative selling weaknesses in it.

The details of the framework are, of course, found in the next chapters, but the basic Jazz! concept works like this.

First, think of a sheet of music with notes on it that indicate which keys to hit on a piano to get the correct melody and rhythm. The Jazz! framework appears on paper as a series of pictures or notes that indicate which elements of a winning presentation to hit, or include, and when to play those elements so that your sales message comes out in the most compelling way possible.

When you were a kid you probably played some kind of instrument (and some of you still play today). Recall a time when you were learning a new song. You were initially dependent on the sheet music to cue you to the correct notes to play. After a little practice, however, you got to know the notes so well that you could play without looking at the sheet music. The same is true with the Jazz! notes. At first, you'll have to look at the pictures to use them. However, you will quickly learn them and be able to play them in your presentations without looking. The result will be the ability to organize your thoughts quickly anywhere, anytime, for *all* selling situations.

There are notes for the introduction to your presentation to get buyers on board and ready to listen to you. There are notes for the middle of your presentation to ensure that you are getting your points across memorably and persuasively. And there are notes for the summary of your presentation to make it as easy as possible for your audience to say yes to your recommendations.

To understand Jazz! in its second use as an assessment tool, imagine that you are playing the piano without any sheet music. You're playing what you think is a terrific rendition of your favorite song. Along comes a professional piano coach who sits down beside you and watches the keys that you're hitting. It's very clear to the coach that you are hitting some wrong notes, going flat in several places, and are off the beat. The coach watches you play, shows you the specific places where you went wrong, and then encourages you to play the song again without the errors.

Jazz! as an assessment tool allows *you* to function like a piano coach. You will be able to look at your presentations and spot where you are hitting wrong notes, going flat with your message, or missing the beat with your buyer. Then you'll be able to fix those weak spots.

Using Jazz! as an assessment tool, you'll quickly see that the notes you hit in your presentations fall into natural patterns. These patterns give you a visual snapshot of the selling power of your presentation. *Strong patterns win business. Weak patterns lose business.*

The fact is, your current presentations already have patterns, only you're not aware of them. By the time you finish this book, you'll have a clear picture of your own patterns, their impact, and how you can enrich and reinforce their power to help you sell even more effectively.

Is Jazz! for Everyone?

Absolutely. Jazz! has worked for salespeople in industries ranging from financial services, telecommunications, advertising, and shipping to engineering, management consulting, executive recruitment, and aerospace. Regardless of your industry, if you have to present to win business, Jazz! will work for you.

It works selling one-on-one across a desk, selling to small groups, and selling in formal large group sales situations. It can be used with all media and visual aids: laptops, handouts, slides, overheads, product demonstrations, or simply a pencil on the back of a napkin over lunch.

It's an innovative approach that replaces traditional hard-to-remember lists of "do's and don'ts." The Jazz! system is:

- *A stress-saver.* It will remove any uncertainty about how to successfully structure a presentation.
- *A time-saver.* You won't have to start from scratch every time you're faced with a new sales presentation situation.
- *A relationship-builder.* It shows you how to sustain that critical personal connection with your buyer throughout the presentation.
- *A charisma-booster.* As you'll see, a side bonus of using Jazz! is that it enhances your personal delivery skills.
- *A business-builder.* Jazz! helps you create the kind of presentations that *move* buyers to say yes.

Three Kinds of Sales Musicians

Sales presenters generally fall into one of three performance categories. In the book, I call them novice, average, and star players. You've seen these presenters yourself at work. Three representatives might all have the same facts and information to sell, but what they do with that information in a presentation can differ drastically.

There are some sellers who, despite their best efforts, give presentations about as compelling and engaging as "Chopsticks." Listening to them, you quickly tune out. Then there are others who are more effective. They're better organized, relate their material back to the audience, and liven up their information with examples. These salespeople do what I call a "perfectly" job—perfectly acceptable, perfectly predictable, and perfectly . . . average. Although technically correct, their presentations lack the sizzle and flow essential to a real connection with the listener. Their presentations are the sales equivalent of Muzak. There is nothing wrong with Muzak itself, but it is not particularly outstanding, memorable, or stimulating.

Finally, there are those whose presentations always seem to catch fire. Organized, relevant, creative, and energetic, they know how to command attention from the outset so that you want to hear more. Their presentations really *move*. They have a rhythm that sweeps buyers along. They tell an exciting, persuasive, and memorable story. And they lead buyers to a close, easily and naturally. Their sales messages are music to a prospect's ears. These are the Jazz! star performers.

Oh, but . . .

"Agghh! I have my own style and personality," you may be thinking. "I don't want to be straitjacketed into any rigid system. Let me out of here!"

Relax.

Jazz music is a uniquely individual medium. The musician brings to it his or her own personality, creativity, style, and judgment. Listen to the recordings of the same song by different jazz greats and you'll hear very different renditions of that song. Duke Ellington, Miles Davis, and David Benoit have very different sounds. Ella Fitzgerald and Billie Holiday were both extraordinary singers but had very different styles.

The same is true in Presentation Jazz! You use its principles to boost the selling power of your recommendations. It becomes as much under your control as any other selling tool, such as your day-timer, laptop, or cellular phone. Ultimately, you may choose to use only some of the principles. That decision is always yours. Regardless of how you use the Jazz! system, you retain *your* personal style, creativity, and judgment. In musical terms, you can play the notes softly or you can pound on the keys. In fact, depending on the selling circumstances, you can become your own arranger. You'll find that the Jazz! system gives you tremendous flexibility and expands your control over the entire presentation process.

An additional bonus of Jazz! is that the more you use it, the stronger and more charismatic your delivery style becomes.

Okay, but How Do I Know These Notes Represent the "Right" Things to Do?

Fair question. Let me answer by asking you to do a brief exercise.

1. Think of a specific situation in which you saw someone give a very effective sales presentation. (It could have been someone presenting to you, a presentation observed on a joint call, or one that you heard in another sales setting.)
2. Recall that presentation. Think of *what* the presenter said and showed (the content and any visual supports that might have been used) and *how* it was said (the delivery). First, describe how you *felt* as you listened to that person.

I Felt

_____

_____

_____

3. Now, jot down what that person *did* in each of these areas to impress you and make you feel that way.

What the Presenter Said/Showed (Content)	*How the Presenter Said/Showed It (Delivery)*
_____	_____
_____	_____
_____	_____

4. Compare your answers to those from salespeople in other industries who have done the same exercise from New York to London, Buenos Aires, Sydney, and Hong Kong.

How Presenter Made Me Feel	*What Presenter Did*
Interested	Looked at me/Didn't read
Important	Had a flow to material
Excited	Moved
Confident	Used hands
Good	Asked questions
Challenged	Related to me
As if she were talking right to me	Spoke at my level
Involved	Used (appropriate) humor
Envious	Varied voice inflection
Engaged	Answered questions well
Entertained	Had professional presence
Worth my time	Spoke with conviction
	Made sense
	Was enthusiastic
	Used examples, stories
	Was easy to follow
	Used visuals
	Seemed to enjoy the experience
	Was creative

Notice how similar your responses are to theirs? Don't be surprised! Getting a message across to someone effectively is a universal, daily human activity. We've all been in enough good and bad communication situations to be able to recognize the differences.

The bottom line is that a strong presentation is *easy to follow* (was organized; had a flow; carried me along), *relevant* (addressed me; related to my needs; spoke to me at my level), *interesting* (used examples; told stories; employed humor; was original in some way; used visuals), *involving* (got me into the presentation; asked questions; used the group), and *energetic* (seller was animated; spoke with conviction; looked at me; seemed to be having a good time; gestured; connected with the audience). All these elements are captured in the Presentation Jazz! system. It's hard to argue that these are not the "right" characteristics of a winning sales presentation.

How This Book Is Organized

Chapters 1, 3, and 5 cover the three parts of any presentation: introduction, middle, and summary. You will be introduced to the notes representing the winning elements for each section. Then, you will see these notes used in a real selling situation as you, the reader, become a buyer and review different versions of the same presentation. Through using these examples, the discussions that follow, and self-tests, you will understand the selling power and versatility of the Jazz! notes system and be able to apply it immediately to your own presentations.

Chapters 2, 4, and 6 highlight the clinkers, or mistakes, that you may be inadvertently making in the introduction, middle, or summary of your presentations, respectively, and provide suggestions for correcting them.

Chapter 7 brings you Jazz! at its liveliest. You'll learn seven different ways to inject creativity into your selling method for truly memorable, persuasive presentations.

Chapter 8 provides quick tips on creating and working with visual aids that apply to both low-tech and high-tech presentations. You'll learn the difference between visuals that aid your sale and visuals that kill your sale.

Chapter 9 reviews the basics all star presenters cover in planning strong presentations. Chapter 10 shows you how to refine your recommendations even further to make them more compelling and memorable. Chapter 11 sensitizes you to the importance of considering buyer and seller communication styles in planning a presentation.

Chapter 12 explains how to control prepresentation jitters. Once you realize that presenting is very similar to playing a sport, it becomes much easier to remain calm in group presentation situations.

Chapter 13 offers strategies and techniques for dealing with all kinds of questions gracefully and professionally. It shows you how to use questions to advance your sale and how to manage difficult questions calmly and confidently.

The Conclusion has some final thoughts on the mystique be-hind winning presentations. Appendix A answers many of the most common presentation questions that I've heard over the years. You'll likely find the answers here to any outstanding questions you may have. (If you don't, please write, fax, or e-mail me at the numbers listed at the end of the book and I will respond.) Appendix B contains all the Jazz! formats and a summary of chapter highlights for quick reference and easy review. You may copy the formats and use them as often as you like for all your future presentations.

One Final Word

Superstar performance, whether it occurs in the concert hall, on the playing field, or in a prospect's office, happens not by accident but by design. Not surprisingly, the best performers are constantly fine-tuning their craft. More than one sports pro, like famous golfer Lee Trevino, has said: "The harder I practice, the luckier I get!" Legendary comedienne Lucille Ball said, "Luck? I don't know anything about luck. Luck to me is something else: hard work—and realizing what is opportunity and what isn't."

Presentation Jazz! is a proven opportunity for you to increase your business. In today's competitive environment, whether you sell products or services, the stakes are increasingly high. Missing the mark is a luxury few salespeople can afford. With Jazz!, you will be able to plan successful presentations with confidence, in *less* time, the *first* time, *every* time. Then, when you present (play) to your prospects and clients (audience), your message (sales music) will earn you their business (applause) over and over and over again (Encore!).

1

Get on the Beat!

How to Use Your
Introduction to Engage Buyers

You are at a party. There are lots of people milling around, talking to each other. You spot someone across the room you want to meet. Of all the conversational openers you might use, would you simply say, "Hi! Your place or mine?"

Obviously, most of us would not take that approach. You'd more likely initiate a conversation that built some common ground or identified a common interest. Then, at the right moment, you'd invite the person out.

Let's reverse the situation. Imagine that someone (not your favorite Hollywood star) you don't know comes up to you at the same party and the first words he or she utters are, "Hi! Your place or mine?" How would you feel? Would you be a bit startled? A bit put off? What would you think of that person? Too fast? Too pushy? Too coarse? Too self-serving?

Introduction dynamics in presentations are not unlike cocktail party approaches. Both aim to engage. One person is trying to interest the other in giving time, attention, and favor. At the party, the context is romantic. In a presentation introduction, the context is business.

You are attempting to engage your buyer, to arouse curiosity, and to heighten interest so that he or she listens to what you have to say. Your attempt is made more difficult because you are competing against every other thing preoccupying the buyer at that moment. Due to intense competition and information overload, breaking through the clutter in your buyer's head is a formidable task these days.

If you rush the engagement process in a social situation, the personal connection never has a chance to occur. Similarly, if you rush the engagement in an introduction, you risk sabotaging the business connection. In both cases, you miss *getting on the beat* with the other person.

Introductions That Engage

While I won't try to advise you on finding romance at your next cocktail party, I can give you the elements of a winning introduction (the *notes* of the *sales music*) to play at your next client meeting so that you and your listener *get on the same beat*. These notes are in the form of pictures or icons, similar to the icons on your computer. See Figure 1-1.

Figure 1-1. The Jazz! introduction notes.

	Buyer's				
Buyer's	Situation	Setup	Idea/	Buyer's	
Objective	and Check	Question	Recommendation	Objective	Transition

Basically, a strong introduction gets the buyer's attention immediately (his objective, ☺ his situation ⌂); bridges (**?**) to a snapshot, or preview, of your idea or recommendation (💡) so that the buyer knows what is coming next; reinforces (☺) the value of that idea or recommendation, which whets the buyer's appetite to hear more; and moves both of you (>) easily into the supporting information, details, and arguments in the middle of the presentation.

The Notes Defined in Detail

 The Buyer's Objective

People care about their own goals and objectives before they care about your product or service. To get their attention, it is strategically smart to "hit" their objective first.

Achieving a goal makes people feel good, so the note for the Buyer's Objective is a smiling face.

Common business objectives are:

- *To increase* some quantity
  (profits, sales, revenues, productivity, shipments)
- *To improve* some quality
  (morale, quality control, performance, response time, efficiency)

- *To achieve* something
  (successfully launch a new product, maximize a budget, have a great sales meeting, maintain a competitive edge, position the company for the twenty-first century)
- *To reduce* some quantity
  (time, error rates, defects)
- *To protect or avoid* something
  (a franchise, market share, liability)

 The Buyer's Situation

The Situation is a brief review of what you learned from your information-gathering discussion with this buyer, which could occur on the same visit, in a telephone conversation, or from a previous in-person call. When you mirror back to a buyer a brief summary of his situation, you create a bond with that buyer. He feels you understand him. You also increase his attention because you are talking about his business.

Since any buyer's situation is likely to contain both *positive (+)* and *negative (−) facts,* which give rise to a *need,* this note is a split smiling/frowning face.

This brief review of the buyer's situation is followed by a checking question to verify these assumptions. That quick confirmation by the seller is indicated in this note by the check alongside the smiling/frowning face.

- The *positive facts* are what's been good up to this point (what's up; what's exciting; what's been working until now) in the buyer's business.

- The *negative facts* are what has gone wrong or is at risk (what's changed; what's under pressure; what's threatening) in the buyer's business.

- The buyer's *need* is the problem or challenge that has to be fixed, solved, or resolved as a result of the negative facts.

Checking question examples include:

• *Have I left anything out?*
• *Is that right?*
• *Has anything changed since we spoke?*

A nonspoken check could simply be a pause, looking at people for their silent nod of agreement.

Buyer's Situation Example:

Mr. Buyer, (+ *facts*) *you've recently expanded your operation and business is booming. However, (− facts) you are experiencing some quality control issues that you hope are temporary, but which are causing a flood of calls to your customer service people, who are not prepared for such a large call volume. As a result, you've lost some major customers. You're taking steps to remedy the problem with an extra sales push, but short term (need) you want to train the staff in customer service to avoid additional loss of customers.* (checking question) *Have I left anything out?*

? *The Setup Question*

This is a quick, but powerful, note to hit in a presentation. It is a *short* question that the *seller* will answer. This question acts as the *bridge* that leads the buyer from his or her world to your recommendation. It *focuses* the entire presentation for the buyer. Because it is a question, it lends a sense of drama to the presentation, as the buyer now awaits the answer.

The obvious symbol here is a question mark. Setup Question examples include:

• *What's your best option?*
• *How can we help?*
• *Why reconsider our proposal?*
• *Why should you change suppliers?*
• *What's the solution?*
• *How can you leverage this success?*
• *How do we add value?*

The Idea/Recommendation

This is a preview, or snapshot, of your main message or recommendation. It is *not* the full presentation. It is the answer to the previous Setup Question.

Since you are presenting an idea, the symbol is the light bulb.

Main messages or recommendations frequently begin with phrases like these:

- *We can help by giving you . . .*
- *The answer is to do the following three things . . .*
- *The incremental value in working with us is that you'll get . . .*
- *Your best option is to do . . .*
- *The reason to reconsider is that . . .*
- *When you work with us, you'll get . . .*
- *The (program/system/direction) we recommend is . . .*

 The Buyer's Objective (repeated)

This is the same symbol as the opening Buyer's Objective. It is used to wrap up your introduction so that you end where you began: with the presentation focused on the buyer's objective.

At this point, you are making a statement about the buyer *accomplishing* his objective, or a statement that captures the spirit of the buyer accomplishing his objective. Linking your recommendation back to the buyer's original objective gives closure to your introduction and whets your buyer's appetite even further to listen to the details of your presentation.

The symbol is, again, a smiling face. Sometimes, this step is a separate thought. Sometimes, it is in the same thought as the Idea. Examples include:

Separate Sentence

- *As a result, this will help increase your profits.*
- *As a result, this will help you meet your objective.*

Stated With the Idea

- *We recommend a two-tier customer service program for telephone operators and supervisors, lasting over a period of three months, (link to buyer's objective) which will help rebuild your business long-term.*

(Generally, it's a good idea to point out that whatever you are recommending will *help* achieve your buyer's goal. Unless you are in a unique situation where you control everything, or are privy to certain information, it is usually risky to absolutely guarantee a result.)

> *Transition*

This is a phrase or sentence that effortlessly carries the buyer along to the supporting information in the rest of your presentation.

The symbol is an arrow to indicate forward movement. Examples of Transition phrases include:

- *Let's begin with . . .*
- *The first thing to look at is . . .*
- *Take a look at . . .*
- *In order to understand this, let's step back and look more closely at the factors behind this situation. . . .*

To appreciate the power of these notes and how they work together, let's play them in an actual presentation. You will see three versions of the same introduction. In each case, imagine yourself as the buyer.

Scenario: You are Alex, a meeting planner in a division of a large corporation, responsible for selecting the annual sales meeting venue. You must also guarantee that everything runs smoothly during the meeting. Your reputation lives or dies by the success of these meetings.

Sixty salespeople who love golf and tennis will be attending. They have gone to different resorts in Florida and Arizona every year with great success. This past year was difficult for the company, but the sales staff turned in superior results, and management wants to show them a particularly wonderful time at this event.

At the moment, you are meeting with Meg, a travel consultant. You spoke with her on the telephone last week and told her about your meeting needs. The conversation was pleasant, and she asked for the chance to present a resort in the Rocky Mountains to you.

Having completed the amenities, she is about to begin her presentation. See Figure 1-2.

Figure 1-2. Meg's first introduction.

Note	Introduction #1
	Alex, I want to tell you about magnificent Rocky Mountain Resort (RMR). I really think it is one of the most outstanding resorts in the country. I love it!

As Alex, how engaging is this introduction for you? How do you feel toward Meg at the end of it? My guess is that you were not particularly grabbed by this opener and that you felt it was a little fast. Are you left with the feeling that Meg is a bit more interested in making her commission than in really helping you?

This introduction is too focused on the seller and the seller's agenda. The buyer feels the seller's enthusiasm, but when the seller rushes headlong to her idea or recommendation, represented by the 🔆, she is ignoring the buyer. The net result is not so different from what you feel in a social situation when the speaker's idea of scintillating conversation is to tell you how wonderful they think *they* are.

This is the novice presenter at work. Far from getting on the beat with her buyer, the sales music in this seller's opening has all the engagement power of "Chopsticks."

Let's try the second version, shown in Figure 1-3.

How engaging is this opener? Better? Definitely! There's a balance between Meg's interests and your interests. At least, she links *her idea/recommendation* (I want to tell you about this magnificent resort . . .) *to*

 your objective: what's important to you ([that] will make your annual meeting a huge success).

Figure 1-3. Meg's second introduction.

Notes	Introduction #2
	Alex, I want to tell you about this magnificent resort in the Rockies called Rocky Mountain Resort. It's one of my favorites, and
	it will really make your annual meeting a huge success this year.

As Alex, you probably feel somewhat more positive toward Meg than you did in Introduction #1.

Introduction #2 is not bad. It reflects some understanding that the buyer's needs are to be brought into the presentation as soon as possible. This presentation hits the notes that most presenters use. Sometimes these notes are reversed; for example:

 Let's talk about making your meeting a huge success this year.

 RMR is a magnificent hotel, etc.

In either order, this is the average presenter at work. The combination of the two notes creates sales music that is like Muzak: not unpleasant, but not entirely a grabber.

Now, for the third and last version of Meg's introduction, see Figure 1-4.

How engaging was this introduction? Do you want to hear more about the resort? How do you feel toward Meg? If you're like most people, you can see that Introduction #3 is more tightly connected to the buyer's needs. The thinking that went into this

Figure 1-4. Meg's third and last introduction.

Notes	Introduction #3
☺	*Alex, it's great to be able to help you make this year's sales meeting the best ever for your staff.*
☹✓	*My understanding is that* • *historically, you've gone to warm-weather resorts* • *you've got sixty people who love golf and tennis* • *last year was a tough one and management wants an outstanding meeting to recognize the extraordinary performance of your people* • *so, the challenge is to find that special place that satisfies everyone without also breaking the bank.* *Did I leave anything out? (No, Meg, that's it.)*
?	*So, how will Rocky Mountain Resort fill the bill?*
💡	*You'll score a home run with it. You'll get all the amenities of the finest warm-weather resorts, the novelty of the majestic Rockies, and recreational opportunities to satisfy everyone. It's a remarkable place*
☺	*that will make your sales meeting one your people will never forget!*
>	*Take a closer look at what you'd get, beginning with the incredible range of activities. . . .*

introduction is far more strategic than the thinking in the first two. The result is much stronger sales music: Buyer and seller are definitely on the same beat.

This is the star presenter at work. Take a closer look at the notes the seller plays in this introduction.

Meg wanted to sell, but she didn't rush. Instead she *led* her buyer to her recommendation. She first played *two* notes to establish common ground and common interest with Alex.

Buyer's Objective. A statement of Alex's objective: what he wanted to accomplish or achieve.

. . . [to] make this year's sales meeting the best ever . . .

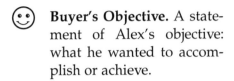 **Buyer's Situation.** A brief review of Alex's situation plus a checking question.

My understanding is that
* *historically you've gone to warm-weather resorts . . .*
* *so, the challenge is to find that special place that satisfies everyone without also breaking the bank.*
Did I leave anything out?

These notes got Alex's attention immediately, since Alex cares first and foremost about his world. (Don't we love people who take an interest in us! Remember the old saying: "People don't care how much you know, until they know how much you care.")

Meg, then, checked her premises/assumptions at this point before proceeding. This Checking Question is important, because her entire presentation is based on the assumption that she had correctly identified Alex's Objective and Situation. Imagine if circumstances had changed suddenly and, for example, Alex had had a budget cut or if management's game plan had changed!

Meg's next note was a short one.

? **Setup Question.** A question to create a bridge from Alex's world to her Idea/ Recommendation.

So, how will Rocky Mountain Resort fill the bill?

Using a Setup Question did three things:

1. It created a natural flow from Alex's world to her recommendation.
2. It gave a touch of drama to her opening by creating in Alex a sense of anticipation for what was coming next. (Meg

could have used a simple statement for the setup: "Here's a place you'll love." However, a statement lacks the dramatic effect of a question.)

3. The short Setup Question focused the presentation for both her and Alex.

Now, Alex wants to hear the answer to the question, which, of course, leads to:

 Idea/Recommendation. A quick overview of what Meg is selling.

You'll score a home run with it. You'll get all the amenities of the finest warm-weather resorts . . .

By waiting until this point to present her Recommendation, Meg was better able to position it as a real fit with Alex's needs.

Meg then replayed:

 Buyer's Objective. Linking back to what got the buyer's attention in the first place.

. . . that will make your sales meeting one your people will never forget!

This made Alex feel even more predisposed toward Meg and highly receptive to what she had to say. The repeated Buyer's Objective, delivered in a matter-of-fact manner, neatly tied up the Introduction. It gave an additional air of strength and authority to the Recommendation.

The final note Meg played moved the presentation forward into its details:

 Transition. A simple phrase to carry the buyer to your first point.

Take a closer look at what you'd get, beginning with the incredible range of activities.

At this moment, Alex is completely *on the beat* with Meg. He is logically and emotionally drawn into what he is about to hear.

Recognizing the relevance and value of what he is hearing, Alex is likely thinking, "Hey, this salesperson is worth my time. She understands me. She is giving me something that will get me what I want. Tell me more." Engagement with buyer is complete. The "head nodding and finger tapping" have begun.

Personal Jazz!

As you can see, the notes form patterns. Strong patterns give power to your delivery skills as well as to your message. Here's a way to prove this to yourself.

Switch for a moment from being Alex (the buyer) and become Meg (the salesperson) and try presenting the earlier Introductions. Say all three Introductions out loud, as written. Feel free to slightly alter the phrasing to accommodate your own style. If you have a tape recorder, tape yourself. (*Tip:* Allow yourself to pause at the completion of each note for emphasis, particularly after the Setup Question.) As you play back the tape, listen for the Introduction that gives you the most authoritative flow and rhythm, or pace.

Clearly, the flow of your thoughts in the third pattern works best not only for your buyer but also for yourself. It lets you be conversational in a simple, unforced way. It *moves.* It carries you and your buyer forward easily into the details of your presentation. It heightens your credibility and professionalism. Most important, it gives you that instant personal connection with your buyer that is so essential to the selling process.

The Jazz! Introduction Format

All the notes you've just seen are organized in Figure 1-5 in a foolproof way for *getting* [you] *on the beat* with your buyers. Down the left-hand side of the figure are the notes and their definitions, which will guide you in playing your best sales music for any buyer. The notes guide you to include the right things in the right sequence and at the right time. To the right of the notes are sug-

Figure 1-5. Elements of a Jazz! introduction.

Notes	
😊 Buyer's Objective	Good Morning . . . (Amenities). What we'll be looking at is a way to . . . Here's how we can help you . . . Our interest today is to help you . . .
🙁 Buyer's Situation & Check	As I understand it, As we know Last time we met, you told me . . . Is that right? Has anything changed?
? Setup Question	Given this scenario . . . In light of this . . . The question is . . .
💡 Idea/ Recommendation	The answer is . . . Our recommendation is . . .
😊 Buyer's Objective	And as a result, . . . Which will . . .
> Transition	Agenda (if appropriate): Questions: ❏ Anytime? or ❏ Hold until the end? Let's begin with . . .

gested phrasings. Customize these phrasings in your own language, following your own personality and style. As printed, they give you a good sense of the logic, rhythm, and flow of a winning Introduction. (*Tip:* It's comforting to know that when you are strapped for time, you can use these phrases and you'll never go wrong. Just fill in the blanks and you'll be right on track with your buyer.)

You'll notice two additional items in the Jazz! format. One refers to *Setting the Agenda* and the other to *Establishing the Procedure for Questions*. These are options that you can decide to include or not, depending on the presentation's objective, length, and formality.

Without an agenda in longer or more complex presentations, you may confuse people as to where your presentation is going. If you don't suggest a procedure for questions, you may not get questions when you want them, or you may get them when you don't want them. As you can see in Figure 1-5, I have not included any icons as notes for them. Just be aware that agendas and question procedures need to be considered in your presentation.

A Jazz! Introduction strategy is applicable to any industry and can be played to fit any style. Look at Figures 1-6 through 1-10, which show the possibilities for the Jazz! approach in *your* business. Two of the introductions replace the buyer's objective with creative openings—another way to grab your buyers' interest immediately.

Figure 1-6 shows an introduction following a brief information-gathering discussion. Casual and conversational, it's a one-on-one meeting.

Figure 1-7 depicts Northwest Advisors, Inc., money managers presenting to Mega-Company, Inc.'s pension fund committee. There are very high stakes involved and it is very formal. They are competing against three other companies, and it is their final presentation.

Figure 1-8 shows a second one-on-one meeting with unexpected time pressure.

Figure 1-9 depicts an advertising sales rep for *Teens Today* magazine presenting to a group of marketing executives at Sports Un-

Figure 1-6. Old pals: one on one.

	S. *Hiya, Alex. How are you?*
	B. *Great, Meg. Haven't seen you for a while. How was your vacation?*
	S. *Terrific. We . . . (Small talk continues.)*
	S. *I know you're beginning to plan for your next sales meeting. Let's see how we can come up with a place for you that will make your meeting a huge success. Bring me up to date.*
	B. *Sure . . . (Buyer and seller go through a probing/ needs discussion. Seller moves into the introduction to her presentation.)*
	S. *So, if I have this right, you want a major blowout this year.*
	B. *Absolutely. It has to knock the sales staff's socks off.*
	S. *We're talking sixty people, golf and tennis lovers all. They're used to warm-weather resorts. Business was a killer last year and senior management wants to recognize the staff's extra effort by doing something different. Is that about it?*
	B. *Don't forget that it can't break the bank.*
	S. *Right!*
	B. *Okay, so what's your best choice?*
	S. *Alex, go with Rocky Mountain Resort. You'll score a home run with it. It's got everything: amenities, the novelty of the majestic Rockies, and enough recreational opportunities to keep your people busy day and night.*
	They will be talking about it for years to come.
	B. *Sounds good, but expensive.*
	S. *That's the best part; it isn't. Take a look for yourself. (Opens the brochure to show Alex.)*

S = Seller
B = Buyer

Figure 1-7. The beauty contest.

	Good morning, everyone. As a money manager, Northwest Advisors appreciates the opportunity to speak to you about your interest in diversifying Mega-Company's portfolio to help increase its overall returns.
	Right now, as we all know, your portfolio is equally weighted between equity and fixed-income investments. The growing returns overseas have become attractive to you, and you are exploring international equity investment for $20 million of your fund. (A pause and a look seeking agreement—silent nods).
	What do we offer?

	With Northwest, you get the advantages of what our clients call P.A.T. service.
	    Performance—we have been in the top tier for the last ten years.
	    Analyst coverage—you'll get the broadest overseas coverage in the industry.
	    Timeliness—you'll get the latest systems and staffing to ensure accurate and prompt reports and service.

	You'll see that Northwest is well positioned to help you achieve your portfolio goals.
	Per your guidelines, we will include a quick review of the company's background, our performance, our investment process, and how we work with accounts. We will be happy to answer your questions at the conclusion of the presentation.
	Let's begin with a brief overview of the firm you'd be working with. . . .

limited, a teen sportswear company. The opening is a creative lead-in to the buyers' goals and situations. Notice how it still leads to the setup question.

Figure 1-10 shows a dramatic opening by an advertising agency that was after the advertising business from a rail transportation company.

Figure 1-8. "You have five minutes!"

S.   Bill, good to see you again. I've brought a wonderful slide show to . . .

B.   Tina, I'm sorry, but I can give you only five minutes, ten max. My boss called an unexpected meeting.

S.   It would be better to reschedule. How about . . .

B.   No, let me hear it now. I have to submit my recommendation today.

S.   Got it. Okay. I reviewed your specs and basically you want to maximize your space.

• Business is booming.
• Staff levels are exploding and will continue to grow.
• You are locked into your current location for the next three years.

Have I left anything out?

B.   Unfortunately, no.

S.   Best option?

Go with the Furniture Flex System. This is a modular system of partitions and desks that creates an attractive environment that's easy to rearrange as your needs change.

Installing this system will meet all your objectives.

I recognize your time is short. What other information do you need from me in order to decide?

In the Spotlight: Your Turn

You've seen the engagement power of a Jazz! Introduction. Now it's time to become your own presentation coach and evaluate the power of your Introductions. You can do this in two different ways. Review the contents of a formal presentation you recently gave, or recall a recent meeting with a prospect/client at which you pre-

Figure 1-9. Creative introduction.

This presentation—by an advertising sales representative of *Teens Today* magazine to a group of marketing executives at the teen sportswear company Sports Unlimited—features a creative lead-in to the buyers' goal and situation. Notice how it still leads to the setup question.

Good morning, everyone. Let me ask you something. If I say "fast food," what name comes to mind? ("McDonald's," says one. "Burger King," says another.) And if I say "sneakers," what's the first thing you think of? ("Nike . . . Reebok," they answer.) And if I say "teen sportswear," what do you think of? (Without missing a beat, they all say, "Sports Unlimited!")

In this room, that's true, but if you asked 90 percent of American teens to name a sportswear line, you know their first answers would be Competitor A and Competitor B. And that's the problem you've identified.

Sports Unlimited makes a terrific line of clothes, but you are losing market share due to:
  * *Increased competition*
  * *Competition outspending it in advertising*

With your new line coming out, you've decided to become more aggressive in your advertising. Right? (Enthusiastic nods.)

So, how can Teens Today help you?

We'll give you the most powerful direct line to your target market. Teens Today is the number-one teen monthly. It's the largest book in the field, with the biggest spenders, and with an editorial environment perfect for your campaign.

Advertising in Teens Today will absolutely help you increase your business.

Take a closer look at these numbers, starting with the size of the market you'd be reaching. . . .

Figure 1-10. A stunt as introduction.

	Mr. Jackson, the senior director (the prospect) from the railroad, arrived at the advertising agency's office and asked to see its senior director, Mr. Smith. The not-very-friendly, gum-chewing operator very slowly dialed the appropriate extension and then, equally slowly, told Jackson to wait in the next room.
	On entering the room, Jackson was appalled to find it dirty and stuffy, smelly from cigarette butts left in the ashtrays, and messy with used coffee cups and newspapers strewn about everywhere. After waiting for five minutes, which seemed like fifteen, in this unpleasant setting, the outraged prospect rose to storm out of the office. Just then, Smith walked in.
	Before Smith could speak, Jackson exploded. "How dare you treat me like this!" he said. "Is this the way you treat your clients? I wouldn't think of doing business with you! Now, if you'll excuse me, I will be leaving."
	"Wait!" Smith said as Jackson bolted for the door. "This was all a stunt. But do you see how upset you are at the way you were being treated? Well, that is exactly how people feel riding your rail system! They think it is dirty, messy, and more late than on time. They are as furious with it as you are with me at this moment!" Jackson, who was halfway out the door, came back, closed it behind him, and listened as Smith apologized for the stunt while at the same time defending it as a much needed eye-opener.
	"Now," Smith said, "Would you like to see the advertising campaign that can help change people's minds about your railroad?"
	Jackson not only agreed to see the campaign; he ultimately signed with the agency.

sented your ideas, services, or products informally. Then, write down what you said in your Introductory remarks *prior* to getting into the selling details that supported your Idea or Recommendation.

For example, if you're a graphic designer and you recently talked to a prospective small-business president who is looking to get new clients, you might remember that you said the following and write: *Mr. Bronson, I can give you a new image in your promotional materials to enable you to compete more successfully for new business.*

Examine what you wrote down. Write, or draw, the appropriate Jazz! notes alongside the different parts of your Introduction.

For example, as you look at the Jazz! notes in Figure 1-1, you will see that your introduction hit these notes:

 I can give you a new image in your promotional materials

 to enable you to compete more successfully for new business.

Your introduction might have many more words than my examples. That's okay for now. Our goal here is to develop your sense for the basic elements of a strong Introduction. Whether the graphic designer said the above as it is written, or she said, *I'm so excited to be here today to talk to you about your new business and to help you improve your promotional materials, which I think are so creative and contemporary, so that you can be the graphic designer name on everyone's lips for every major corporation in the city!*—the fact is she still hit the Idea note followed by the Buyer's Objective note.

Here's another example. If you sell sales force automation software, you might remember calling on a vice president of a Fortune 500 company and saying the following:

> Last time we met, you told me that while business is good, you worry what will happen when this cycle ends, which at some point it must. Your key concern is that you are technologically behind the competition, and you've got to get a sales force automation system in place quickly in order to be more responsive to your clients.
>
> My firm has designed sales force automation software for companies like yours many times, and I know we can help you. We can offer you A . . . , B . . . , and

C . . . , which will help you manage your sales processes much more effectively.

Again, you would see that your Introduction hit these Jazz! notes:

   Last time we met, you told me . . . clients.

   My firm . . . can help you. We can offer you A . . . , B . . . , and C . . . ,

   which will help you manage your sales processes much more effectively.

These notes reveal the selling pattern of your Introduction. Compare your pattern to the three patterns in Figure 1-11 to assess its selling power.

Which pattern does your introduction most resemble? The pattern you select tells you how, consciously or unconsciously, you approach presentation introductions. Your pattern is a strong indicator of how well you engage buyers at the beginning of a presentation.

Looking at your pattern of notes, be your own coach and use the answers to these questions to decide which changes you would recommend to yourself to improve the selling power of future introductions.

The answers to these five questions will help to highlight the relative strengths and potential weaknesses in your presentation introductions.

☐ *Do you tend to begin with your Buyer's Objective and Situation and, then, Check () that they are correct? Or, do you typically rush right to your Idea or Recommendation ()?*

If the latter is true, you must be the "Hi! Your place or mine?" person from that cocktail party! You are failing to connect with your buyer, both on a business level and on a human level.

If you omit the checking question, you may find yourself going off track in your presentation.

Figure 1-11. What kind of sales music are you playing?

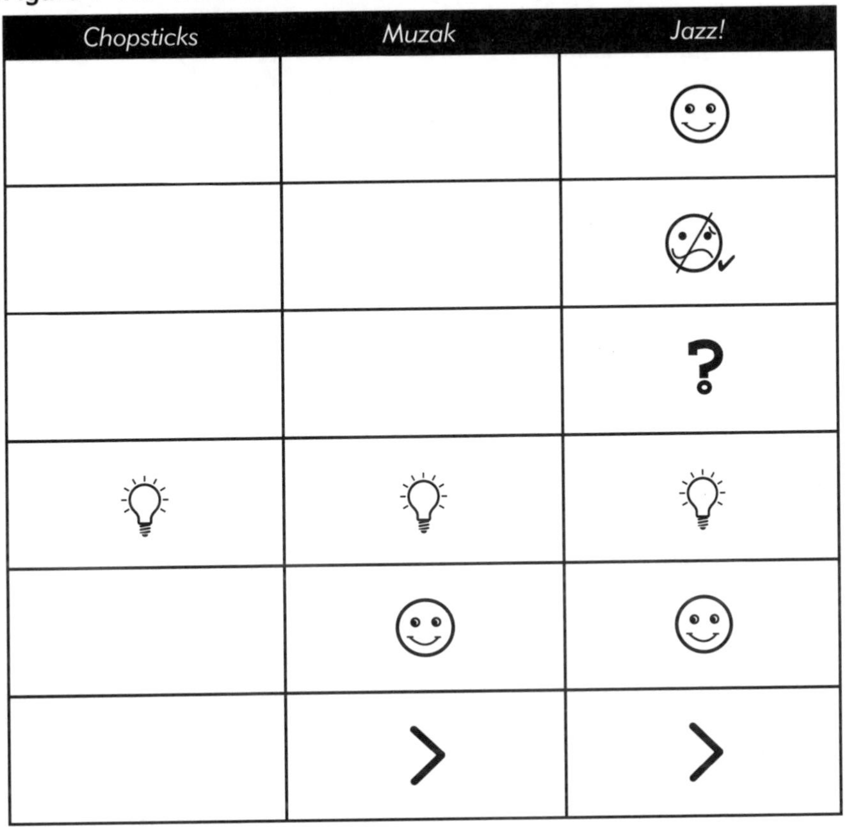

Chopsticks	Muzak	Jazz!
		☺
		⊘
		?
💡	💡	💡
	☺	☺
	˃	**˃**

☐ *Do you tend to include a short Setup Question (**?**) prior to your recommendation?*

Most people miss this one. However, without it, you're missing an opportunity to add some theater to your introduction, to focus your presentation more strongly, and to lead your buyer naturally to your Idea or Recommendation.

☐ *Do you tend to state your Idea or Recommendation (💡) clearly and succinctly?*

If not, your client may become confused as to exactly what you are recommending and, even more important, how it meets his needs.

☐ *Do you tend to link your Idea or Recommendation back to the Buyer's Objective (☺)?*

If not, you're missing an opportunity to further whet your buyer's appetite for the detailed selling points that are about to come.

Also, you miss wrapping up the introduction and may not sound as authoritative and professional as you would like.

☐ *Do you tend to Transition (❯) smoothly to the information in the middle of your presentation?*

If not, there may be an awkward "dead space" between your opening remarks and the information in your first detailed selling point.

Polish Up Your Star!

If the sales music in your introductions is at the level of anything less than a star performer, you should rethink how you approach and plan your introductions. What notes, or elements, do you want to change, add, or modify? For example, if you realize that you tend to open with what *you* want to sell rather than focusing on the *buyer's* world, then you will want to change your approach and open with a focus on your buyer's Objective and Situation. If you realize that your introduction comes to an abrupt end, then you will want to add an appropriate Transition phrase to smoothly move into the Middle of your presentation.

Make those changes to the introduction you just analyzed. Use the Jazz! introduction format in Figure 1-5 to guide you. Rework your opening until you are satisfied. Remember, the notes are merely directional signals, prompting you to sequence your thoughts in a winning way. The *how*—your language, your phrasing, your delivery—is up to you.

When you're done, say your new introduction out loud. Better yet, tape-record both the old and the revised versions and play them back. Your second introduction should sound much more engaging to you.

Oops! Are You Hitting Clinkers?

If your introduction seems to be hitting all the right notes in the right sequence, but you're still not wildly enthusiastic about the sales music it's producing (and you can't figure out why), you may be hitting *clinkers*, common Introduction errors. In the next chapter, we'll examine them. But first, let's summarize what we've covered so far.

Summary

1. An introduction, which can be as short as a minute but not longer than several, is a critical part of the sales presentation. At its conclusion, your buyer is either engaged or uninterested. He's either on the beat with you or he's tuned you out.

2. Star presenters understand that winning introductions are

- *Buyer-centered*
- *Structured* to capture the buyer's interest and lead easily, naturally, and powerfully to the more detailed information in the selling points to follow

3. The Jazz! notes capture all the elements of a winning introduction. They follow the sequential pattern in Figure 1-1.

Hitting these notes in your introduction will have your buyers eager to hear more of what you have to say.

2

Clinkers

Common Introduction Mistakes

"Say what's on your mind, Harris—the language of dance has always eluded me."

With any set of skills, whether in sports, music, or sales presentations, there are always subtle elements in the execution that contribute to superior performance. When these elements are slightly off, they undermine the results. See if you are inadvertently undermining your presentation with any of these sales *clinkers*.

Wrong Focus

This is the overuse of first person pronouns and phrases: the "I" word and its related phrases. These put the focus of your comments on you, the seller, when the focus should be on your buyer. Examples include "*I* think . . . ," "*My* company has . . ." "*We* have . . ." "*ABC* (the seller's product) does . . ." The effect on your buyer is no different than it would be on you in a social situation. The *over*focus on the seller and the seller's products or services and the *under*focus on the buyer will make your buyer tune out completely.

Solution

Switch your pronouns to the second person as often as you can: "*You* get . . ." "*Your* people will . . ." The change in pronouns draws buyers into your message and draws them closer to you personally. See Figure 2-1.

Figure 2-1. Focusing with the use of pronouns.

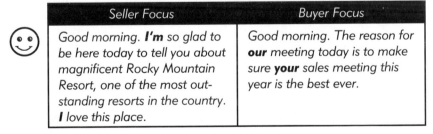

	Seller Focus	Buyer Focus
☺	Good morning. **I'm** so glad to be here today to tell you about magnificent Rocky Mountain Resort, one of the most outstanding resorts in the country. **I** love this place.	Good morning. The reason for **our** meeting today is to make sure **your** sales meeting this year is the best ever.

The unfortunate irony of this clinker is that it usually stems from your strong enthusiasm for what you're selling. But product knowledge and gung ho attitudes backfire when they exclude the buyer and the buyer's interests. Look at your Introduction. Is it focused on the buyer or the seller?

Weak Idea or Recommendation

We live in an age of overcommunication. The average adult is exposed to over seventy thousand messages a year from television, magazines, radio, and newspapers alone. Is it any wonder that buyers have a hard time absorbing and remembering all the stimuli coming at them from all directions, including your sales message?

Think about it. How many automobile commercials do you remember? How many cereal commercials stick out in your mind? Very few. Between television, the Internet, direct mail, faxes, online services, 50-plus cable channels going to 500, newspapers, magazines, advertising on everything from blimps to supermarket carts, race cars, sports tournament banners and stadium stands, the insides of taxicabs, and (yes!) bathroom stalls, buyers are on *message overload*. There was even the suggestion to put advertising on satellites to be visible from the earth—truly shopping with the "stars."

Due to this communication explosion, your idea or recommendation, even if passionately presented, is very likely to get lost unless it can break through the clutter. This is even more true when competition for your product or service is strong.

You must strike a chord with your message in your buyer's mind to ensure a memorable, meaningful, and motivating Idea/Recommendation. The best way to express that idea is in vivid language that will instantly link, or hook, the concept of what you are selling into an already familiar mental image in your buyer's mind. This link to something already familiar to your buyer increases the chances that he will instantly understand and remember what you are selling. These hooks often use imagery or a catchy phrase.

Imagery is the use of comparisons (metaphors and analogies).

A metaphor directly compares the meaning and attributes of one thing to another. For example:

- *Life* is *a bowl of cherries.*
- *This problem* is *just the tip of the iceberg.*

In presenting, someone selling advertising space might say her publication *is the hot line to her buyer's best customers.* In our example with Meg and Alex, Meg was telling Alex that he would *score a home run with Rocky Mountain Resort. Hot line* and *score a home run* are concepts immediately understood by most buyers.

Everyday business language is filled with imagery: high grossing products are "cash cows," top executives are "hotshots," competitive advantages are "secret weapons," the business environment is a "jungle" or "dog-eat-dog" world, distributors have a place in the "supply chain," rising profits "lift all boats," disadvantaged companies are "behind the eight ball," stock markets "nosedive," investors are "bulls" and "bears," and the high-tech area south of San Francisco is "Silicon Valley."

An analogy is a more involved comparison. It uses similarities between two things or situations to explain an important point. For example:

- He was like the wind. *He blew into town quickly and just as quickly blew out!*
- Building a relationship is like building a house. *Without a firm foundation, both will collapse.*

In presenting, a computer salesperson might say that the service contract he is offering is like an insurance policy. *You don't want to have to use it, but it's good to know that it's there.*

A catchy phrase is an explanation that is easy to remember. It generally has a rhythm to it. For example:

- An overnight delivery firm salesperson might offer *service on time, every time.*
- A software development company salesperson might offer

T.A.D.: Tailoring to your needs, Attention to detail, and Delivery as promised.

If you look at business-to-business advertising in publications such as *Business Week, Fortune,* and *Forbes,* you will see that many of the most memorable and effective advertisements use imagery or catchy phrases to instantly "hook" their main message into your mind. Compare the two sets of recommendations in Figure 2-2.

Figure 2-2. Using imagery or catchy phrases.

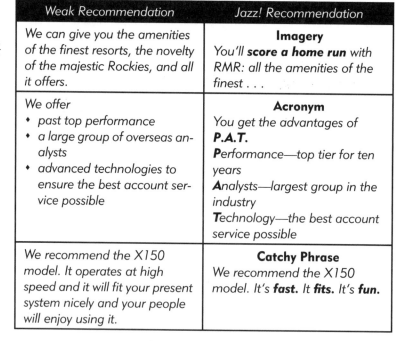

Weak Recommendation	Jazz! Recommendation
We can give you the amenities of the finest resorts, the novelty of the majestic Rockies, and all it offers.	**Imagery** You'll **score a home run** with RMR: all the amenities of the finest . . .
We offer • past top performance • a large group of overseas analysts • advanced technologies to ensure the best account service possible	**Acronym** You get the advantages of **P.A.T.** **P**erformance—top tier for ten years **A**nalysts—largest group in the industry **T**echnology—the best account service possible
We recommend the X150 model. It operates at high speed and it will fit your present system nicely and your people will enjoy using it.	**Catchy Phrase** We recommend the X150 model. It's **fast.** It **fits.** It's **fun.**

Most salespeople don't think of sharpening their ideas or recommendations with hooks, but you can see how hooks give extra sales appeal to a message. They are short. They are easily understood. They are easy to remember. They are often visual. They contain the essence of your entire recommendation in a few words. (If you are using visual aids, reinforce your words with an actual picture or graphic of your hook.)

How to Find the Hook for Your Presentation

Take the central thought in your Idea or Recommendation and mull it over. Talk through the answers to these questions: *Why* are you recommending this idea? *Why* is your product or service right? *Why* are you better than the competition? *What is the product or service that you are recommending or selling comparable to?*

Note the verbs and nouns you use to answer those questions. Let your mind free-associate a bit. The hook will come to you. For example:

- Is what you are selling going to *bridge a* marketing *gap* for your buyer?
- Will it give the buyer a chance to *get in on the ground floor?*
- Will it give the buyer a *turn-key operation?*
- Will it protect the buyer *like an insurance policy?*
- Are you offering the buyer a *package* of features or benefits?
- Are you providing *an umbrella system* for all the buyer's needs?
- Does your recommendation *cover all the bases* of the buyer's concerns?
- Are you selling *pinpoint precision?*
- Does your idea *hit a type of target* for the buyer?
- Is the buyer getting *the look of a Rolls Royce at the price of a Ford?*

In the act of talking your idea through, you will invariably come up with the hook. If you do this with a colleague, you are likely to develop even stronger hooks.

In a recent seminar, a consultant was looking for a hook to strengthen the sticking power of his recommendation, which was basically to use his company for the management of a project. He found his hook quickly using this method. First, we started to talk through his idea out loud. I asked him why his prospect should select his company over the competition. He thought about it for a moment and answered, "Our professionalism, experience, and our many services." (Not bad. It has a certain rhythm to it, but it's also a pretty predictable Idea.) Then, I pushed further and said that surely his competitors could, and would, say the same thing, so why was his company really better? Without thinking, he blurted out, "Because we're like architects! We design the whole project and manage it from start to finish, which most other companies do not do." We liked this architect image and played with it a little more. I said, "If you're like an architect, what does that make your competitors?" He thought about it for a minute and said, "Well, it makes them more like just the workmen, like carpenters."

Bingo! he had his hook. His Introduction then played itself out like this:

 Mr. Client, you want to accomplish . . .

 Right now, you're facing . . .

 How can we help?

 Basically, unlike most other companies that will play a specialist's role, similar to the role of a carpenter, we will be your architect. *We will design your whole project from start to finish, ensuring greater control and quality consistency throughout.* (In the corner of his slide would be a picture of an architect's blueprint.)

 As a result, your project will be completed the way you want it, with no surprises.

The rest of his presentation then reinforced the carpenter-versus-architect theme.

With a little practice, you will be able to express your ideas in stronger language to hook your recommendations into buyers' minds.

Strengthening Your Recommendations

Compare the examples in the following table. The weak versions in the left-hand column are juxtaposed with stronger Jazz! recommendations on the right. Almost all the examples, both weak and strong, are accompanied by visuals. Although a well–thought-out visual can bolster the language of a recommendation, a weak visual is as ineffective as weak language. On the other hand, even if showing visuals is not possible for some reason, a recommendation with vivid language will strengthen the sticking power of your message in your buyer's mind.

Weak Recommendation	Jazz! Recommendation
I recommend World Printing Inc. (Picture of printing press)	*Replace your current services with World Printing, Inc.—the Tiffany of the industry.* (Picture of printing press set in a diamond)
Use our T-730 model. It's fast, efficient, cost-effective, and everyone in sales and operations will be able to use it. (Picture of T-730 model)	*Use our T-730 model. It's fast, efficient, cost-effective, and will do double-duty for you: Everyone in sales and operations will be able to use it.* (Picture of weight lifter holding up a barbell with sales at one end and operations at the other)
I recommend Money Manager X. They have an outstanding international investment performance record. (No picture)	*I recommend Money Manager X. Their strong international performance will round out your investment portfolio.* (Picture of a completed investment circle)
I recommend we do a needs analysis first. Then, we design a system to fit those needs. Then, we'll implement that system. Then, we'll monitor it and refine it where necessary. (A visual that says XYZ System)	*I recommend our total four-step package that consists of needs analysis, design, implementation, and follow-up monitoring and refinement.* (A visual with a package labeled XYZ and the four components as bullets)
The answer is Office-Ez Integrated Software—the latest flexible multiservice software. (A picture showing the software package)	Slay those big-company Goliaths with your own David—*Office-Ez Integrated Software—the latest flexible multiservice software.* (A picture showing the client as David, standing over the slain Goliath competition)

Weak Recommendation	Jazz! Recommendation
Use our Superior Account Management System. It's the most popular one in the field today. (No picture)	Leapfrog *the competition with Superior Account Management System. It's the most popular one in the field today.* (Picture with client leapfrogging the competition)
You've done well with us. I recommend that you expand and renew for next year. (No visual)	*You've done well with us.* Leverage a winner! *Expand and renew for next year.* (A visual that shows winning with your product, for example, a blue ribbon, a finish line, or the Olympic logo)

Revisit your introduction. What changes can you make in your Idea or Recommendation to make it hook more easily into your buyer's mind and increase its selling power?

Rambling

This occurs when you go on, and on, and on—and on. Rambling kills the rhythm of your presentation, undermines the logic behind your selling message, and bores a buyer. If they're not careful, salespeople can ramble in every note of the introduction.

Solution: As with perfume or cologne: *less* is better. Although the Introduction is critical for setting the stage, it is meant to be brief. Think in bullet points, not dissertations. Your urge to tell more will be satisfied later, when you get into the middle of your presentation. See Figure 2-3.

Since communicating styles vary among people, you may prefer the music of the rambling examples. The question, though, is will your buyers also like them or will they tune you out? If you've seen one too many glazed-over expressions in your buyers' faces during a sales call, you might want to think about crisping up your introductions a little more carefully in the future. Look at your current introduction. Does it need a little tightening up in any note?

Figure 2-3. Rambling vs. Jazz!

Rambling	Jazz!
Good morning. We want you to have a very successful sales 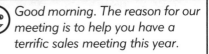 meeting this year, with all the bells and whistles—a meeting that will make every other one pale by comparison. Why, I remember a meeting a couple of years ago when everything went wrong, the food was bad, the accommodations were tacky, and the service was appalling. And then there was an unexpected storm that destroyed the golf course! You can't imagine what a mess that was. No, we want a place that is foolproof and fun.	Good morning. The reason for our meeting is to help you have a terrific sales meeting this year.

You'll be inviting about sixty people. Some of them have been with you for as long as twenty years. That's amazing in this day and age with all the takeovers and mergers. Anyway, you usually go to warm-weather resorts for these events, like Florida, Arizona, or southern California. Business was tough last year. I understand you really got killed with foreign competition, not to mention the currency fluctuations last spring. But the good news is you pulled through. Some of your folks like . . . Did I leave anything out?	I understand: • You've got sixty people who like to play golf and tennis. • You've always gone to warm-weather resorts. • You had a particularly tough year and you want to recognize the staff with a special locale this year. Did I leave anything out?

(continues)

Figure 2-3. (Continued)

Rambling	Jazz!

So, what can RMR do for you to make sure that your folks feel rewarded for the great job they did during such a tough last year so that you will have a memorable meeting?

So, how will RMR fill the bill?

You'll get all the amenities of a warm-weather resort, like tennis, golf, and beautiful weather. We average 82 degrees in the summer. You'll also get the beauty of the Rockies. You should see the peaks at sunrise and sunset! Also, people can fish, hike, hang glide, soar, swim, and balloon.
Also, . . .

You'll score a home run with it. You'll get all the amenities of a warm-weather resort, the novelty of the majestic Rockies, and a wide range of activities to delight your staff.

As a result, you will have the best time ever, what with all the activities, and the scenery, and the food, and the service, and . . .

As a result, people will have the best time ever.

Tentativeness

People use words like *if, perhaps, might, maybe, could, suggest, I think,* and *I believe* to be polite, but the unintended consequence is to raise doubt in your buyer's mind that what you are saying is true or will work.

Solution: Eliminate the *I think*s and *I believe*s (unless you, personally, are asked your opinion), or, at least, keep them to a bare minimum. Replace qualifiers with words of certainty like *when, will, recommend.* See Figure 2-4.

Exception: In certain industries, it is illegal to guarantee a result. For example, in the securities industry, a broker cannot say, "We recommend stock ABC. It *will* go up." However, a broker can say, "We recommend stock ABC. We're projecting a potential 20 percent increase in its value by year-end."

Look at your introduction. Do you use tentative phrases? When you eliminate as many of these as possible, your buyer will have more confidence in your ideas.

Self-Assessment

Now, consider your overall introduction again. Think of your past presentations. Think of any feedback you may have gotten from colleagues, managers, or customers. Which clinkers might you be habitually hitting in your Introductions? Which would you like to work on?

Clinker	Not a Problem	Needs Work	High-Priority
1. Wrong Focus (too many "I" pronouns & phrases)	___	___	___
2. Weak Idea or Recommendation (missing a hook)	___	___	___
3. Rambling			
A. At the Buyer's Objective step	___	___	___
B. At the Buyer's Situation step	___	___	___
C. At the Setup Question step	___	___	___
D. At the Idea step	___	___	___
E. At the restated Buyer's Objective step	___	___	___
4. Tentativeness (sounding Unsure)	___	___	___

Figure 2-4. Tentative vs. Jazz!

Tentative	Jazz!
If you install this system, I think, hopefully it might save you $250,000.	When you install this system, it will help save you up to $250,000.
At RMR, I believe you will have a terrific time.	At RMR, you will have a terrific time.

Jazz! Up Your Introduction

Tape your revised introduction. Play it back until you're satisfied that the clinkers are gone and that it has the strongest possible sales appeal to a potential buyer. When you reach that point, congratulate yourself. You're playing introduction Jazz!

With a winning introduction behind you and your buyers eager to hear more, you're ready to move into the middle of your presentation. Chapter 3 shows which notes star presenters play to transform data, facts, and information into an exciting, flowing, and persuasive sales story.

3

Now You're Cookin'!

How to Get Your Selling Points Across in the Middle of Your Presentation

There's a proverb that says, "When I tell you, you forget. When I show you, you remember. When I involve you, you understand."

For example, if I wanted to sell you on trying the game of tennis, I could just *tell* you about the game. "Tennis is played on a 78-foot-long court. One or two players stand on either side of the court. The game is played with racquets and a tennis ball. It's a very exciting game." I could *show* you a video of what I'm talking about, which would help you see how the game is played and would also get you to feel the excitement of it. I could also *involve* you by getting you on a court, putting a racquet in your hand, and playing the game with you, giving you a chance to experience it directly. Clearly, telling, showing, and involving would be better than just telling you about the game. Telling is basically all information. Showing and involving add feeling, emotion, and excitement to the information.

People remember only 20 percent of what they hear, 50 percent of what they hear and see, 70 percent of what they say, and 90 percent of what they say and do. Star presenters understand that "cookin' with buyers," or driving points home, depends on presenting information in the way that people absorb and retain information best. Telling is not enough. Showing and involving are needed to make the sale.

Hitting the Right Notes

You'll notice something very different about the notes that represent the winning elements in the middle of a presentation. They occur in a mixed pattern, unlike introduction notes, which, as you saw in Chapter 1, run in a definite linear, or sequential, pattern. That sequential order reflects the purpose of an introduction: to get your buyers to want to hear more. Therefore, introduction notes *lead* a buyer into your presentation.

However, the purpose of a presentation's middle is different: It is to *explain* the specifics of your idea, *excite* your buyer about that idea, and *persuade* him or her of the value of that idea. Your facts, details, and explanations are the core of your presentation, but the other notes dance in and around that information to create the excitement and persuasive power of that information. Since your information varies with each buyer, the pattern of notes will also vary with each presentation. See Figure 3-1.

Figure 3-1. Jazz! middle notes.

| Information | Key Buyer Point | Word Picture | Involvement | Transition |

These notes ensure that your information points (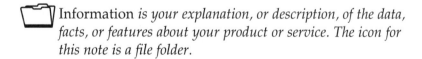) are relevant (**!**), interesting (⊕), involving (⟳), and flow together smoothly (**>**). They will appear in a varied pattern. They add life, color, meaning, excitement, rhythm, and movement to your presentation. Working together, those notes make what would otherwise be dry information "sing" for your buyer.

The sequence of notes isn't as important here as it was in the introduction or will be in the summary. It is the *presence* or *absence* and *mix* of these notes that will determine your selling power.

The Notes Defined in Detail

Information *is your explanation, or description, of the data, facts, or features about your product or service. The icon for this note is a file folder.*

Information generally includes facts that describe what you're recommending, how it works, your experience, how much it costs, timing, and any other necessary details. These are examples of information:

+ The system takes two months to install.
+ We take the team approach to servicing your account.
+ Your programs are tailored to your needs.
+ We have over two hundred satisfied clients.
+ Three million people read our publication.

- The car has antilock brakes.
- Our technology offers a new array of image-manipulation and document-handling options.
- Our investment process works like this . . .

! The Key Buyer Point (KBP) *is the benefit of that information to your buyer, or the conclusion to be drawn from that information. You can also think of the KBP as the take-away, the punch line, or the "So what does this mean for the buyer?" Since the KBP is the "point" of the information to the buyer, its icon is an exclamation point. You may have several benefits associated with your information. Generally speaking, though, at the end of a block of information, you will have a primary Key Buyer Point.*

KBPs as benefits make your information relevant to the buyer. Phrases that trigger Key Buyer Points include: *which gives you . . . , bottom line, you get . . . , which means you can . . . , this allows you to . . . , so, you'll be able to . . .*

KBPs as Benefits

- It costs . . . *so you enjoy a savings of $ . . .*
- The system does . . . *which will reduce waste by 32 percent.*
- You'll need only one person for this, *which frees up personnel for your special projects.*
- The equipment has . . . *so you'll never have to worry about downtime.*
- You get maximum braking and steering control on slippery roads with model . . . *which assures you maximum safety.*

KBPs as Conclusions

- The competition is introducing a new product in thirty days, *so your window of opportunity is less than a month.*
- Your error rate is . . . *Again, you need to replace your equipment.*
- Both tests failed, *so, bottom line, you are left with only one option.*

Benefits or conclusions can be said before, after, or before and after your information to form a kind of "key point sandwich":

- *Your people will have a wonderful time.*
- *Attendees can choose from many activities, including, tennis, hiking, golf, and ballooning.*
- *Bottom line, there's something to satisfy everyone at RMR.*

Tip: While it is good to have a mix of benefits and conclusions appearing in the different positions (beginning, end, beginning and end), if you are going to state the benefit or conclusion of a piece of Information only once, state it at the end. It will definitively drive your point home, particularly if your Information is complex, and it will always make you sound more authoritative than if you leave the benefit or conclusion unstated.

 Word Pictures *are* words that create pictures *in buyers' minds. They help buyers see, feel, understand, and retain your Information. The beauty of Word Pictures is that they make complex information simple and simple information meaningful. They make your Information lively and interesting. The icon for a Word Picture is a picture frame inside a person's mind. It is generally a good idea to have at least one Word Picture for every different piece of Information that you present.*

Word Pictures fall into three categories:

1. Examples or stories.
   - We have more than two hundred clients, *such as IBM and GTE.*
   - *Let me tell you what we did for AT&T . . .*
2. Comparisons (metaphors and analogies).
   - *You don't want to be roadkill on today's information highway.*
   - Entering this market will make us *the big fish in the little pond.*

       • They go together *like rhythm and blues.*
       • Rejection bounces off them *like bullets off a Sherman tank.*
       • *A woman is like a tea bag. You never know how strong she is until she gets into hot water. (Eleanor Roosevelt)*
       • *Minds are like parachutes. They work best when open.*
       • Trying to compete without a marketing strategy *is like going off into the woods without a compass. You are going to get lost.*

3. Concrete numbers. These are abstract numbers that are translated into something familiar to the buyer. Numbers are meaningless abstractions. They have impact only when compared to something else—another number, an equivalent amount of time or resources, or another known human situation.

    Examples are:
       • It costs $925, *half the cost of last year.*
       • The ideal consumer has $ . . . household income, a house valued at $ . . . , and a clothing budget of $ . . . *In short, we are talking about the Macy's customer, not the Kmart shopper.*
       • We reach 1,000,000 readers. *That's ten Super Bowls of potential buyers for your product.*
       • A gigabyte can store a billion characters, *roughly the equivalent of one thousand average-size novels.*
       • We're talking a billion dollars, *enough to operate every school in America for five hours.*
       • Your investment would be only $200,000. *You have a staff of thirty. If each one made one extra call a week for forty weeks, that would be 1,200 calls. If you figure a 20 percent close rate, that would be 240 more sales. Your average sale is $2,000. That works out to $480,000. This would more than pay for your $200,000 investment in sales force automation.*

4. Quotations/testimonials. Quotations from people or sources known to buyers increase the credibility of your information because they validate what you're saying:

- *GE's* . . . division said our system increased its sales by 15 percent.
- Is a team-building program necessary? *As John D. Rockefeller said, "I will pay more for the ability to get along with people than for any other ability."* You bet it is!
- Automobile Magazine *rated XYZ automobile number one for the year.*

You've seen the definitions and some isolated examples of Word Pictures. Figure 3-2 shows the difference in selling power when these Word Pictures are added to your basic Information.

 Involvement *draws buyers into the experience of what you are presenting. It keeps people engaged with your Information. The icon for this note is a pair of circular arrows, suggesting continuous involvement between buyer and seller.*

There are several ways to involve your buyers.

1. Personalize your remarks: Use "you" and "your" pronouns; refer to your buyer directly.
2. Mental involvement: Ask people to estimate, imagine, or think about something; use rhetorical questions:
   Imagine the following . . .
   Think how you feel when . . .
   Let's take your department, for example . . .
   How do we do that?
3. Actual involvement: Ask for a response:
   Does that make sense?
   Are we on the right track?
   What do you think the financial department will say?
   How does this compare to your past experience?
   Which of these options would you like me to discuss first?

In Figure 3-3, compare the difference in impact when the salesperson moves from doing a monologue to actively involving the buyer.

Figure 3-2. Telling vs. telling and showing.

Telling (Information)	Telling & Showing (Word Pictures)
Example	
We offer many activities for your staff.	We offer many activities for your staff, including hiking, soaring, golf, tennis, fly-fishing, and ballooning.
Story	
We're able to respond to all problems to give you a hassle-free meeting.	We're able to respond to all problems. Last summer, a keynote speaker took ill the night before her big speech. She was able to reach her doctor back east, and we filled her doctor's prescription. The next morning she was perfectly fine and incredibly grateful to us for helping her out. Whatever it is, we're committed to giving you a hassle-free meeting.
Comparisons & Analogies	
Information is coming at us very quickly. We have to manage it.	Information is coming at us very quickly. It's like drinking water from a fire hose. If we're not careful, we could drown.
Bruce Burns will be handling your business. He is a very talented person.	Bruce Burns will be handling your business. He is the Michael Jordan of the industry.
Concrete Numbers	
The cost is $X per attendee.	The cost is $X per attendee, which makes the total cost for your meeting about half the price of one of the systems your company sells.
(To a shopping center executive) You'll save 40 basis points on this deal.	You save 40 basis points on this deal. That's enough to build a new shopping center in the Caribbean.

Quotation/Testimonial	
We recommend you do the audit now, when times are good.	As John F. Kennedy said, "The time to fix the roof is when the sun is shining." *We recommend you do the audit now, when times are good.*
We get rave reviews from clients and media.	*We get rave reviews from clients and media.* Gillette said we were their most responsive supplier. *Business Week* called us the best-managed company in our industry.

Transitions give momentum and forward movement to your presentation. Transitions connect points, highlight special information, and act as minisummaries to increase retention of your key selling points. Transitions make it easy for your buyer to follow your Information. The arrow icon for Transitions is the same icon used for transitions in the introduction.

Transitions are used:

1. To connect points
   * *In addition . . .*
   * *On the other hand . . .*
   * *What about . . . ?*
   * *Another benefit is . . .*
   * *Moreover . . .*
   * *Now, let's turn to . . . Not only do you get X, but you also get Y.*
2. To highlight information
   * *If you think . . . was important, wait until you see . . .*
3. As a minisummary
   * *So far, you've seen that this system meets your needs, is easy to operate, and is cost-effective. Now, how will we make it happen?*

Figure 3-3. Telling vs. telling and involving.

Telling	Telling & Involving
Personalizing	
This place is great.	You'll *love* this place.
We have lots of activities.	You said you wanted a *fun time* for people. With all the activities we offer, your people *will have* more choices than time to enjoy them.
I think the views are breathtaking	What you get *are breathtaking* views.
We will completely schedule the day for your group from morning exercises to evening entertainment.	Let's look at how your group might spend its day . . .
Mental Involvement	
The day begins with an optional exercise class in our glass-walled studio.	Imagine the following: *you wake up, put on a pair of shorts, and a T-shirt. In two minutes you are exercising while looking at a 360-degree view of some of the most breathtaking scenery in the world.* That's what it's like at RMR every day.
We help with all audiovisual problems.	Think about *your worst audiovisual nightmare.* With our full-time A/V staff and state-of-the-art equipment, that will never happen at RMR.
There are nine gourmet restaurants.	You've traveled a great deal. How many gourmet restaurants would you expect in a small town like . . . (short pause). Well, *if you guessed nine, you're right!* (It doesn't matter if your buyer was thinking of a different number. If he guessed lower, he's impressed

| | *with nine. If he guessed higher, nine still is a good number for a small town. If he was thinking nine, he feels smart for having guessed right. The question was not offered as a test, but as a way of mentally involving him in a selling point.)* |

Rhetorical Question

Now, let me tell you about the facilities.	What about the facilities?

Actual Involvement

There are lots of activities to do, such as golf, tennis, and ballooning.	There are lots of activities to do. How many people do you think would sign up for each of the following?
You get value, unique activities, and great views. In terms of A/V support, we offer . . .	*You get value, unique activities, and great views.* How does this sound? (Pauses for buyer's response). *You'll also like our AV support.*

Information liberally mixed with Key Buyer Points, Word Pictures, Involvement techniques, and Transitions results in presentations with great selling power.

Putting the Notes Together

We return now to the meeting with the travel consultant from Chapter 1. As you look at the three examples that follow, notice which presentation notes are played and which aren't, the variety in the note patterns, and the effect the different patterns have on you, the buyer. (You may notice that two notes can be played in a single sentence.)

Scenario: The travel consultant has just said to you, "Take a closer look at what you'd be getting . . ."

In the presentation in Figure 3-4, the seller hits the Information note almost exclusively and creates a data dump. Also, notice that

Figure 3-4. Hitting the Information note almost exclusively.

Notes	Presentation #1
	This conference center has ten meeting rooms that all face out to the mountains.
	When they're not working, people can take advantage of lots of wonderful outdoor activities, like tennis, biking, soaring, golf, and ballooning.
	Our price includes all meals, one free lesson, taxes, and gratuities. The price is $ . . . per attendee.
	We have state-of-the-art audiovisual facilities as well.
	Also, our chef is really terrific.

the operating pronouns are seller-focused: "we" (the resort) and "our" (the resort's).

This is a novice presenter at work. The pattern of the notes she plays is not very interesting. Novice presenters tend to recite their Information without Word Pictures. They are running so hard on their own track that they don't take the time to think of the right Word Picture to help their buyers to better "see" and understand what they're saying. The result is a boring grocery list of easy-to-forget facts that blur in the buyer's mind. This seller and her message create sales music that has very little persuasive power. After listening to a presentation like this, it is not unusual for the buyer to say, *Thank you. We'll get back to you.* Don't hold your breath!

The presentation in Figure 3-5 is somewhat better. The seller helps the buyer a little more to see what he or she is talking about. There is more of a focus on the buyer by using pronouns like "you" and "your."

Figure 3-5. An average presentation.

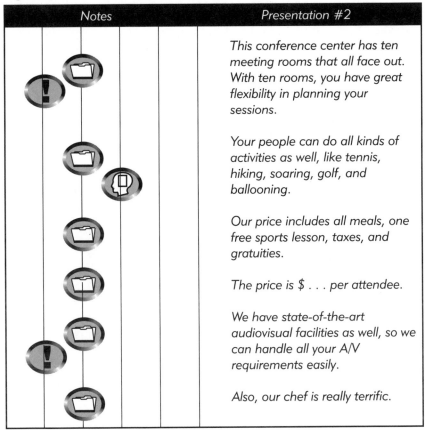

This is an average presenter at work. The pattern of the notes in this presentation has a bit more variety to it. However, average presenters tend to use the same Word Pictures for all their presentations. They tell the same stories and use the same examples. They often don't use analogies tailored to the buyer or to the numbers that have been made concrete for the buyer. Very often, they come across as "canned." Such a presentation is a bit more relevant and interesting to the client than the novice's, but it makes only moderate impact. Like Muzak, you're aware of it but it doesn't stay with you.

Most people would pick the presentation in Figure 3-6 as the

Figure 3-6. A star-quality presentation.

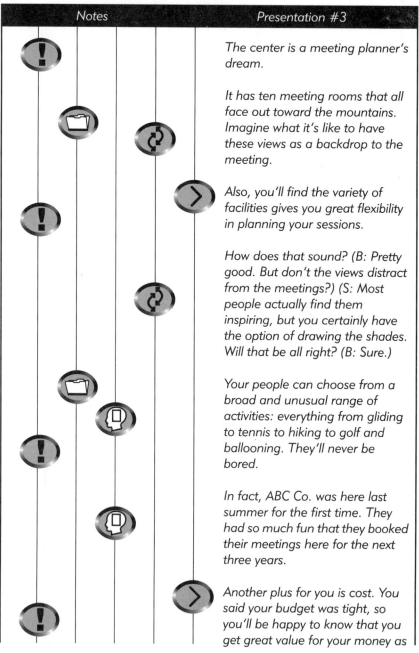

well at RMR.

Included in your price are all meals, one free sports lesson per participant, and all taxes and gratuities. Bottom line, it's everything you need in one place.

The price is $ . . . per attendee. For sixty people, that is less than half the price of one of the widgets you sell.

In addition to value, great facilities, and lots of recreational choices, you get hassle-free audiovisual support.

We have state-of-the-art A/V here. You can do anything from simple overheads to computer presentations to video conferencing, which is important since you said your A/V demands were pretty complex. Right? (B: Yes.)

Last, but not least, you will be very pleased with the cuisine. Our chef is famous in the area for his superb cooking. Critic X gave him a rave review again in Gourmet Living.

Of course your group has guaranteed seating at every meal, so dining arrangements are a breeze.

And you know how important the food is at a resort for people? (B: Right!)

one with the greatest selling power. It isn't that the third presentation contains more information, but that the addition and mix of notes that are played with the Information sell it more successfully.

This is a star presenter at work. This presentation *tells, shows,* and *involves.* It paints pictures for the buyer, makes the information relevant, and involves the buyer in the process in many ways. Last, it is totally buyer-focused, with a liberal use of *you* and *your* pronouns.

Star presenters approach every presentation as if it were the first time they were giving it. They think about that particular buyer and will use all the Word Picture and Involvement techniques available to them to make their Information come alive for the buyer. Yes, they may use some of the tried and true stories and examples that have appealed to other buyers in the past, but they also spend time developing just the right *new* ones to drive their selling points home in the most effective way possible for a particular buyer.

This presentation reflects the thinking, planning, and execution of a Jazz! presenter.

Personal Jazz!

Again, what works for the content in your presentations also works for your personal delivery style. Switch and become the travel consultant presenting the three previous examples. Say each one, as written. Notice which one produces a natural conversational flow and an easy rhythm or pace. Notice in the third presentation how your voice takes on added intonation and interest. Notice how the key points, particularly the ones occurring at the end of a block of information, give authority and punch to your delivery. Notice how the other notes in that third presentation add interest and momentum to your message. Use your tape recorder to really hear the differences.

Figures 3-7 and 3-8 are two other examples from different industries of these notes in action.

Figure 3-7. Selling welded grating to a purchasing agent at a steel company who needs grating for a walkway around a population area.

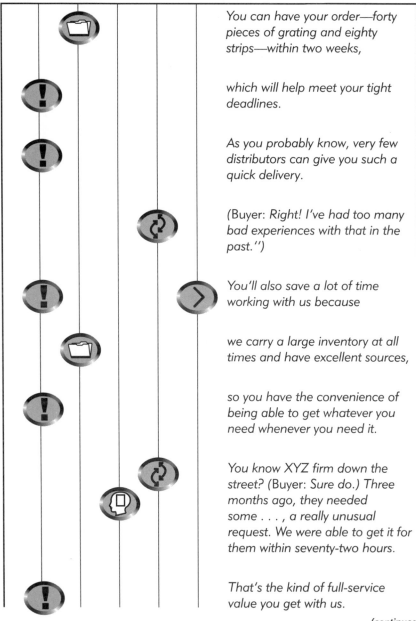

You can have your order—forty pieces of grating and eighty strips—within two weeks,

which will help meet your tight deadlines.

As you probably know, very few distributors can give you such a quick delivery.

(Buyer: Right! I've had too many bad experiences with that in the past.")

You'll also save a lot of time working with us because

we carry a large inventory at all times and have excellent sources,

so you have the convenience of being able to get whatever you need whenever you need it.

You know XYZ firm down the street? (Buyer: Sure do.) Three months ago, they needed some . . . , a really unusual request. We were able to get it for them within seventy-two hours.

That's the kind of full-service value you get with us.

(continues)

Figure 3-7. (Continued.)

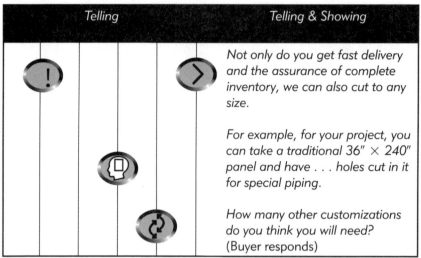

Telling	Telling & Showing
	Not only do you get fast delivery and the assurance of complete inventory, we can also cut to any size. For example, for your project, you can take a traditional 36" × 240" panel and have . . . holes cut in it for special piping. How many other customizations do you think you will need? (Buyer responds)

How to Create Your Own Sales Music: "Improvise"

The notes in the middle of a presentation move your message forward in a varied pattern and will be different for different buyers. It's like improvisation in jazz. The musician keeps the beat and the rhythm of the piece but plays the notes differently to suit the mood at that moment. As a presenter, you keep that beat and rhythm by focusing on your buyer. Playing the various notes differently around that focus to appeal to each buyer creates the sales music that gets your buyer excited about buying.

This is not as difficult as you might think. In your everyday conversations with colleagues and friends, you are already sensitive to the need for these notes. How many times have you listened to someone and thought, *What is the point here?* (Aren't you looking for the Key Buyer Point?) Or *I don't understand what that means. I wish she would help me see what she's talking about!* (What is that but a desire for an example?) Or *Boy! This is complicated. I'm confused.* (Isn't this a plea for a helpful analogy?) Or *So, is that number a good return or an average return?* (Wouldn't you appreciate it if the speaker put his or her abstract return into something concrete for

Figure 3-8. Selling printing services to a publishing company.

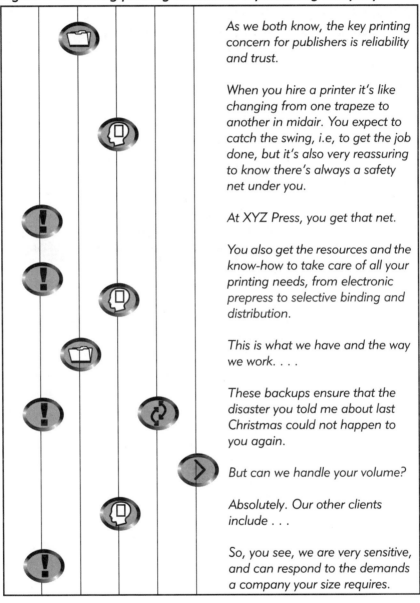

As we both know, the key printing concern for publishers is reliability and trust.

When you hire a printer it's like changing from one trapeze to another in midair. You expect to catch the swing, i.e, to get the job done, but it's also very reassuring to know there's always a safety net under you.

At XYZ Press, you get that net.

You also get the resources and the know-how to take care of all your printing needs, from electronic prepress to selective binding and distribution.

This is what we have and the way we work. . . .

These backups ensure that the disaster you told me about last Christmas could not happen to you again.

But can we handle your volume?

Absolutely. Our other clients include . . .

So, you see, we are very sensitive, and can respond to the demands a company your size requires.

you?) Or *I'm getting lost. Where are we?* (Isn't that a cry for a mini-summary?)

Second, when conversing with friends, family, and colleagues, you make key points and use word pictures, concrete numbers, and transitions all the time. How many of the following do you do in everyday conversation?

_____ You talk in Key Buyer Points (benefits and conclusions):

- Joe, buy the gray suit. *It makes you look ten pounds thinner.*
- Bottom line, kids, if you want to see TV tonight, you have to clean up your room.

_____ You use analogies to drive your point home:

- Trying to get an answer from Joan *is like trying to nail Jello-O to a wall. You can't pin her down!*

_____ You always use examples to illustrate what you mean:

- I want to move to a warmer climate, *like Arizona or Florida.*

_____ You tell stories:

- Sue, your experience with your boss is like mine. *When I started, I remember . . .*

_____ You translate abstract numbers into concrete terms:

- $3000 for the complete computer setup? *Wow! I can recover that in only three business assignments.*

_____ You use quotations and testimonials for credibility:

- Bob, you know what they say. *A bird in the hand is worth two in the bush. I would take their job offer.*
- Tony, I'd recommend the Braxton Inn in Napa Valley. Travel World *magazine had a great review of it.*

_____ You involve others:

- Honey, I really like the red car. *What do you think?*

_____ You use transitions:
- Bill, *not only* was the game great, *but we also* had the best seats! It was a terrific day with the kids.
- *All right, let's see where we are.* You've packed the luggage. I've got our passports and traveler's checks. You have the tickets. We're ready to go.

If you're presenting in an informal situation where you're explaining your products or services, bring these elements that you use in everyday conversation into your selling conversations. As you explain your information, think: *What can I do to help my buyer see my information more easily? What can I do to involve him in what I am saying? What is the key buyer benefit or conclusion of this information?* and *How will I transition from this block of information to the next block of information?*

In situations in which you have time to prepare in advance, ask yourself the same questions. (We'll cover planning in greater detail in Chapter 9.)

After a while, this approach to a presentation becomes automatic. You can do it without looking at the notes. A bare-bones flow of a strong presentation is shown in Figure 3-9. This is a sample outline of a hypothetical presentation. The buyer works for ABC Company and the seller represents Company X. The actual informational details have deliberately been left out. You can imagine the specific facts. In reviewing this stripped-down presentation a few times, it is more important that you get a feel for the elements (notes) and flow (melody) that results in buyers wanting to say yes to your recommendations.

With a little practice, playing these notes will become as natural to you in business as they are in talking with friends socially. The result will be presentations with a stronger logical flow, more satisfying listening rhythm, and compelling emotional pull that will set your buyers whistling your tune.

Figure 3-9. Bare-bones flow of a strong Jazz! presentation.

Notes	Sample Presentation Flow
	ABC will be able to save $ . . . with product X.
	It costs . . .
	These costs can be changed, depending on . . .
	So, bottom line, this is a good investment.
	What do you think?
	Not only are you saving . . . but you are also getting . . .
	The . . . works like this . . .
	For example, . . .
	It's similar to . . .
	which, again, makes it extremely efficient.
	Earlier you said. . . . You'll be pleased to know
	. . . that the staff requirements are only . . .
	Imagine what that would do for your . . .
	so you see it really is easy to implement.
	How does that sound?

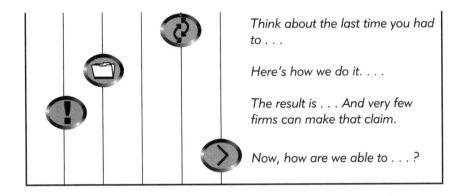

In the Spotlight: Your Turn

If you are in sales, then you most likely play many of these notes in your presentations already. The real question is, Are you playing them as well as you can? Are you producing presentation Chopsticks, Muzak, or, Jazz!? It's time to become your own coach again and find out how Jazz!y the middle of your presentation is.

Use the same sample sales presentation from your world that you chose in Chapter 1. Select three pieces of information that you used or would normally use to support your recommendation or idea in that presentation. (For example, how your product or service works, how it compares to competition, what it costs, and your track record.)

There are two different ways to run your sales music test. You can write out your presentation or put it in short bullet-point form. There are also two ways to score your presentation. One way is to write in the appropriate notes alongside what you wrote.

The second way is to mark the middle of your presentation using different colored Avery dots. Let red dots stand for Key Buyer Points, green dots for Word Pictures, blue dots for Involvement, and yellow dots for Transitions. As you walk through your presentation, put the appropriately colored dots on each page to reflect the presentation elements you are using with that information. When you have finished "dotting" these pages, look at the pattern of colors that you have created. Is it monochromatic or does it look like a rainbow? For example, if you have a preponderance of red dots, the good news is that your presentation is probably very relevant. The bad news is that it may not be very interesting or easy to understand and you need to look for places to add examples, analogies, stories, and involvement techniques. If you are missing yellow dots, then you may have a very choppy presentation and need to add in more Transitions.

Examples of the same presentation in both written out and notes format are provided in Figures 3-10 and 3-11 to guide you with your own presentation. In this presentation, the person is selling sales seminars.

Listen to yourself on audiotape as you give your presentation. How convincing is your presentation? How interesting do you sound? Now, return to your written presentation. Look at the pattern of the elements you've included with your Information. Compare the mix of *your* notes to the three patterns in Figure 3-12.

Which pattern does your presentation most resemble? The pattern you select reveals the sales music you generally play. That music is a strong indicator of how well you are getting your message across to buyers.

Are You "Cookin' " on All Burners With Your Buyers?

Whatever your pattern is, opportunities likely exist for strengthening its selling power. Consider the following:

☐ **Is your overall pattern varied?**
  Yes? You probably give lively, interesting, relevant presentations and sound pretty good in the process.
  No? Your presentations are potentially boring.
☐ **Do you use a lot of Key Buyer Points?** ❗
  Yes? Your buyers see the relevance to their world of what you are saying and will pay attention.
  No? You are probably not very convincing.
  Ask yourself, *What does each piece of Information mean to the buyer?* Or *Why will my buyer care about this?* If you can't answer these questions, then either make that Information mean something or get rid of it.

Figure 3-10. Option #1: writing out your presentation.

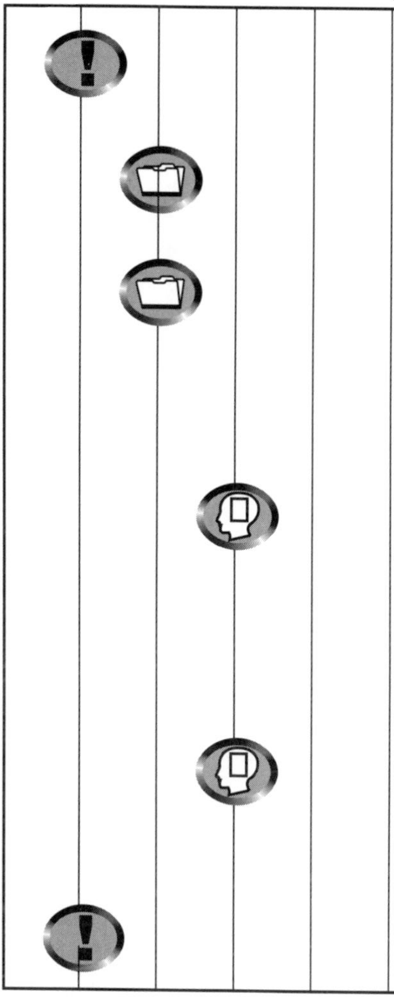

My programs are extremely practical for your people

because they are tailored to your company's specific needs.

We initially interview your personnel, do a needs analysis, and then design an appropriate program.

For example, at XYZ Company, where they constantly found themselves in competitive situations, what they called "beauty contests," I designed an intensive, videotaped two-day seminar followed by individual tutorial sessions.

At ABC Company, however, the focus needed to be on building people's stage presence and the program was a series of short sessions, which gave participants multiple opportunities to practice.

So, anything I do for you will be specific to your needs.

☐ Do you have a liberal amount of Word Pictures in the presentation?

Yes? You are most likely interesting, easy to understand, and easy to remember. Your buyers get it on an emotional level, as well as on a logical one.

No? Your presentations are probably clinically correct but without life—dull and easily forgotten. And so, most likely, are you!

Figure 3-11. Option #2: writing the same presentation in note form.

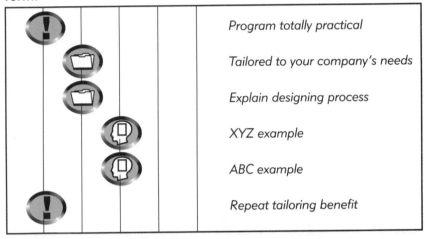

	Program totally practical
	Tailored to your company's needs
	Explain designing process
	XYZ example
	ABC example
	Repeat tailoring benefit

Figure 3-12. What kind of sales music are you playing?

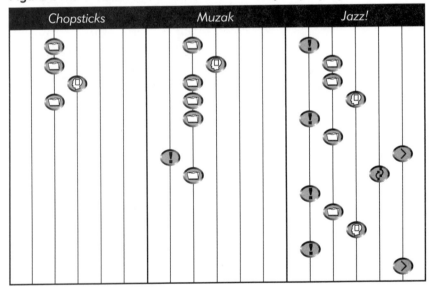

☐ Do you tend to Involve buyers in your presentation? ↺

> Yes? You're helping your buyer participate in the sale by sublimi-
> nally experiencing your product or service.
>
> No? You are doing a monologue and may lose your buyer's
> attention without realizing it, or you may be talking about some-
> thing he or she doesn't want to hear.

☐ Do you use Transitions? ›

> Yes? You make it easy for your buyer to understand and move
> through your Information.
>
> No? Your presentations are probably choppy. There is no
> thread holding your story together.

Polish Up Your Star!

You've seen your pattern. Now identify the elements you want to
change. Where do you need to add or sharpen Key Buyer Points
(benefits or conclusions for the buyer) to make your Information
more relevant? Where do you want to add Word Pictures (examples, stories, analogies, numbers translated to something concrete,
quotations, or testimonials) to make it easier for your buyer to see,
understand, and remember your points? Where can you Involve
(use "you" pronouns, ask questions, and involve mentally) your
buyer? Where do you need to add Transitions (between points or
minisummaries) to smooth out the flow of your Information?

Make those changes to the presentation that you just analyzed.
Then, mark your changes by putting in the appropriate notes
alongside them. Look at how the addition of those notes changes
the pattern and improves the selling power of your message.

Say your new presentation out loud. Better yet, tape yourself
and then listen to the tape. Rework the notes in your presentation
until you are satisfied with the result. Remember, the notes are just
diagnostic; they tell you which elements are, or are not, present in
your presentation. The language you use, your phrasing, and your
delivery are all your own.

Sound better? More persuasive? More interesting? More compelling? Congratulations! Now you know which notes *you* need to

mix into the middle of your presentations for maximum selling power.

Oops! Are You Hitting "Clinkers" Again?

If you seem to have a strong pattern in the middle of your presentation, but it still sounds somewhat off-key, you may be hitting some clinkers. We'll examine these in Chapter 4.

Summary

1. The middle of a presentation is where you get the chance to really *cook* with your buyer. At its conclusion, your buyer is either tapping his fingers and nodding his head (excited and persuaded to buy what you're offering), or he has tuned you and your message out.

2. Assuming you offer good information about your product or service—and most reputable companies do—your success at selling it will depend on the different presentation elements (notes) you play with that information to make it come alive.

3. Remember, people recall only 20 percent of what they hear, 50 percent of what they hear and see, 70 percent of what they say, and 90 percent of what they say and do. Therefore, the notes you play should reflect the way people listen and absorb information. Those notes can be seen in Figure 3-1.

4. Bottom line, a rich and varied pattern of notes produces sales music that wins business.

Now, let's get rid of those clinkers.

4

Clinkers

Common Mistakes in the Middle of a Presentation

"That dog is trying to tell us something."

Think about how you react to the sound of fingernails being scratched across a blackboard. That unpleasant reaction can be the unintended effect you have on buyers when you hit sour notes. Consider the following solutions to produce a sweeter sound for your buyer's ears.

Wrong Focus

There's the story of two people having a conversation and all the first person does for ten minutes is talk about himself. Sensing that his listener is getting bored, the talker says, "Enough talk from me. I'd like to hear about you. So, what do *you* think of *me*?"

That imbalance in a conversation is at the root of two wrong focus clinkers in a presentation. In the first, the salesperson talks too much about herself and her product or service, while leaving out the most important person in the sale, which is the buyer.

In the second, the salesperson makes a claim, assumes the buyer accepts it, and moves on to the next point. Very unwise. Buyers believe what *they* think and say, not what the salesperson thinks and says.

Solution A: Every time you feel the urge to voice your own (obviously biased) view, restrain yourself! Simply change the thought to a question.

Solution B: Convert seller-centered statements to buyer-centered ones. Remember, "you" is the nicest sales word to a buyer in any language.

Solution C: Use stories about other clients, not about yourself. (See Figure 4-1.) Look at your presentation. Are your statements buyer- or seller-focused?

Missing Key Buyer Points

If you have finished speaking and your buyer is left thinking *So what's the point?*, you've hit a clinker. The buyer misses the rele-

Figure 4-1. Seller focus vs. buyer focus.

Seller Focus	Buyer Focus
I think *the scenery is beautiful and people will love it!*	*The scenery is beautiful and people will love it!* What do you think?
	(If he agrees, you have succeeded in bringing him into your unfolding story. If he disagrees, you will get the chance to deal with an objection in real time.)
I think *the views are fabulous!*	Wait until you see the views! They're fabulous!
We have *wonderful cuisine.*	You get *wonderful cuisine.* (or)
	Another plus is that your people will enjoy *wonderful cuisine.*
RMR has *lots of activities.*	*Earlier, you said that* you want people to have *fun in the afternoons.* Well, they'll be able to *choose from lots of activities, such as . . .* (or)
	Past guests have said *that the variety of activities at RMR made it a highlight of their stay.* (The "you" is the identification buyers have with other buyers.)
You say you are reluctant to change locales. I know just what you mean. For years, I had gone on holiday to the Southwest and then a friend convinced me to go to RMR and I just loved it. You will, too!	*You say you are reluctant to change locales. Company XYZ felt the same way. They had always gone to the Southwest and then they came to RMR. They liked it so much they have booked three more meetings here.*

vance of your information to his world. This usually happens when you leave out the Key Buyer Points of your features and facts.

Solution: Always link a Key Buyer Point to your Information. Compare the examples in Figure 4-2. Look at your presentation. Are there Key Buyer Points for all your Information?

Unnecessary Information

Imagine someone walking into your office and reading the telephone directory to you. Your first thought might be, *Who needs to know all this?* And your feelings most likely would be, *This is a waste of my time.*

Unfortunately, you do waste your buyer's time if you confuse a data dump of information with selling. How do you determine what information to include?

Solution: For each set of data, facts, or information you want to present, ask *Why does the buyer need, or want, to know this?* If you cannot answer that question, then leave this information out. For example, the travel consultant from our resort example decides to tell you how RMR was built. Why? Does she think you were an architect in a former life? Doubtful. No matter how interesting that

Figure 4-2. Key buyer points.

Key Buyer Points! Missing	Key Buyer Points! Included
You can choose from ten meeting rooms, which gives you ten different configurations.	You can choose from ten meeting rooms, which gives you ten different configurations, which means tremendous planning flexibility for you.
We have a great chef, which is why he has been written up so much.	We have a great chef, which is why he has been written up so much. So you don't have to worry about people complaining about the food.

RMR history is, unless there is a compelling buyer-centered reason to include it, it would be better for her to skip the architectural history in her presentation.

Voltaire said, "The secret of being a bore is to tell everything." Look at your presentation. Is there any unnecessary information in it that you could eliminate?

Right Information, Wrong Order

1-2-3-5-4 and B-C-A-E-F are sequences that are obviously out of order. Another clinker occurs when your Information is out of order. Buyers have a hard time following you and eventually tune out.

Solution: Always put yourself in your buyer's shoes and check that the order of your Informational points is the best one for that particular buyer. After you discuss your first point, is the next one what the buyer would expect to hear? And the next? And the next?

For example, suppose I tell you in the introduction of a presentation I make that my seminars can help you increase your sales. Of all the things that I could choose to say, how would you advise me to sequence the following supporting Information?

(Put **1** next to the first logical item, **2** next to the next logical item, and so on.)

_____	a. how I would administer the seminars
_____	b. my background
_____	c. my other clients
_____	d. how I tailor the seminars to your group
_____	e. how my seminars compare to the competition
_____	f. suggestions to management for follow-up
_____	g. the results
_____	h. cost
_____	i. a description of the seminars
_____	j. other

Cost is a special issue. It is generally a better strategy to build value, interest, and excitement for your product first, before you discuss final costs. However, discussing cost first can be the right thing to do when it is part of a deliberate strategy to enhance the appeal of your product or service, or to set buyer's expectations. For example, if you are selling a premium priced financial service, you might say, *Mr. Buyer, this is the* most *expensive accounting service on the market and hundreds of clients pay these fees because of the superior, comprehensive service they get working with us. Let me tell you about that proprietary service in greater detail. . . .*

Look at your presentation. Is the order of your information correct for your buyer?

Choppy Rhythm

When you watch professional ice skaters, part of what you admire is their ability to vary their movements and to flow smoothly from one movement to another. If you sound choppy during an otherwise strong presentation, it could be that the pattern of your information and key points is too repetitive and too unvaried, and that the flow between your points is missing.

Compare the presentation patterns in Figure 4-3.

The pattern on the right reflects a presentation that moves and has an engaging rhythm to it. It's a mix of Information, Key Buyer Points, and Transitions between points. The Key Buyer Points sometimes appear at the beginning of the Information and sometimes at the end. The pattern on the left reflects a presentation that is predictable and choppy, without an engaging rhythm. It's a steady pattern of Information, Key Buyer Point, Information, Key Buyer Point, Information, Key Buyer Point—correct in content but boring to the ear.

Look at your presentation. Is there a varied pattern of Information and Key Buyer Points? Do points flow smoothly one into the other with Transitions?

Figure 4-3. Comparison of presentation patterns.

(Read all of column 1 first and then read column 2.)

Canned	Mixed
You have ten meeting rooms, which gives you flexibility in planning sessions.	You have ten meeting rooms, which gives you flexibility in planning sessions.
You'll find state-of-the-art audiovisual equipment, which ensures hassle-free logistics for you.	Moreover, logistics at RMR will be hassle-free for you because you'll be using state-of-the-art audiovisual equipment.
Included in the price are all services, rooms, and meals, which is a great value for you.	In addition to meeting flexibility and peace of mind, RMR is very cost-effective. One price includes all services, rooms, and meals.
	And by the way, our award-winning chef ensures that your people will rave about the food. Bottom line, no matter how you look at it, you get great value with RMR.

Rambling

We all know people who will tell you how the watch was made when you ask them for the time. In any part of a presentation, going off on tangents or overtalking a point loses a buyer's attention. Be honest with yourself. Do you tend to overtalk or overexplain your information, examples, and stories?

Solution: Ask yourself how much the buyer needs to know about this point. Then limit your details to his or her interest level.

Tape yourself to see where you might be rambling and then edit yourself, or dry-run your presentation with a friend or colleague.

At the very least, if you think you have lingered too long on an explanation and you don't quite know how to get out of it, end it with a phrase such as *So, therefore . . .* or *So, bottom line . . .* Either of these phrases will get you out of the ramble and, like a rubber band, snap you back to a Key Buyer Point. Then you'll be free to move on to the next block of information.

A cousin to rambling is verbal overkill, which is using several words when a few will do. (See Figure 4-4.)

Listen to yourself on audiotape. Do you ramble? Are you guilty of verbal overkill? How can you make your message crisper?

Self-Assessment

Consider your presentation again. Think of past presentations. Think of any feedback you may have gotten from colleagues, managers, or customers. Use your answers in Figure 4-5 to determine which clinkers, if any, you might be hitting. Fine-tune your presentations by eliminating these errors.

Return to your presentation. Use the results of your self-assessment test to make your changes until you are comfortable that you are playing the sales music that really *cooks* with your buyer.

You've succeeded. Your buyer is interested. He sees the value of your product or service. He likes what he hears. The time is right to move to the action step.

Figure 4-4. Verbal overkill vs. verbal crispness.

Verbal Overkill	Verbal Crispness
We are in the age of extraordinary international digital communication and interaction.	We are on the information superhighway.

Figure 4-5. Fine-tuning your presentation.

Clinker	Not a Problem	Needs Work	High Priority
1. Wrong Focus			
Self-serving statements	___	___	___
Too many "I" pronouns	___	___	___
Self-serving personal stories	___	___	___
2. Missing Key Buyer Points	___	___	___
3. Unnecessary Information	___	___	___
4. Right Information, Wrong Order	___	___	___
5. Choppy Rhythm			
Repetitious patterns	___	___	___
Absence of transitions	___	___	___
6. Rambling			
Overtelling	___	___	___
Overtalking	___	___	___
Overexplaining	___	___	___

5

"Jazz Is Music That Moves People!"

How to Use a Summary to Move Prospects and Clients to "Yes!"

Look at the circle in Figure 5-1. How do you feel looking at the circle? Would you feel better if the circle were closed? (Go ahead. No one's looking. Take a pencil and close it.)

Figure 5-1. Open circle.

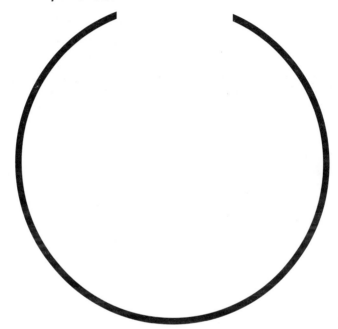

Your initial reaction to looking at the unclosed circle is not unique. People have a strong need for closure. Most of us don't like things incomplete, out of whack, or unbalanced. If you see two pictures on a wall and one is lopsided, isn't your impulse to fix the crooked one to get it back into balance? When you see a person who has one jacket lapel up and one down, don't you have the urge to fix the lapel that is out of place—even if you don't know the person? Think of your desk. What do you do when it becomes so messy that you can't function anymore? First, you stop working. You may even leave the room! But eventually you return and re-arrange the papers into manageable piles so that you are able to work productively again.

All of these examples illustrate the basic principle underlying success in the summary of a presentation.

- People need and appreciate order, balance, and closure in their lives.
- Buyers are people.
- Star presenters satisfy their buyers' need for a complete sense of closure at the conclusion of a presentation.

Summaries That Lead to a Natural Close

Figure 5-2 contains the elements (notes) that will help you satisfy the need for closure. Summary notes are similar but not exactly identical to the notes you play in an Introduction. However, the notes do run in a *sequential* pattern, just as they do in an introduction.

Basically, you end where you began, with a very brief reference to what's most important to the buyer, which is his situation . You briefly restate your Idea or Recommendation ♡ to lock it into his mind, then link it back to him, achieving his objective ☺, which creates a positive feeling on his part as you move to the next step ☐.

The Notes Defined in Detail

 The Buyer's Situation

This is a *very brief* bullet-point recap or all-encompassing statement. You are saying this just to get you and your buyer back on

Figure 5-2. Closing notes.

Buyer's   Idea/   Buyer's   Next
Situation   Recommendation   Objective   Step

track and focused on his world. The icon is similar to the Buyer's Situation icon from the introduction, but without the checking question.

It is frequently triggered by these starters: *In summary, you want . . .*

In summary, we began by saying that you're facing . . .

In summary, your major challenge is to . . .

 Your Idea/Recommendation

This is a *brief* recap of what you have recommended. The icon is the same light bulb from the introduction. A nice option is to briefly list the top three highlights of your recommendation. These can be facts or benefits or both. Three is a magic number. It is easy to remember and pleasant to the ear. We often speak in threes: A-B-C; 1-2-3; Tom, Dick, and Harry; red, white, and blue; bacon, lettuce, and tomato; "I came. I saw. I conquered."

The recap of your Idea/Recommendation is frequently triggered by starters such as:

What you've seen is that XYX Company can . . .

Your best option is to . . .

Our recommendation is . . .

With XYZ Company, you get . . .

The thing to remember about this recommendation is . . .

Your solution is to . . .

 Buyer's Objective

This note links your Idea/Recommendation to his or her original goal. The icon is the same as the Buyer's Objective from the introduction.

It is frequently triggered by starters such as:

As a result, this will help you . . .

. . . which will help you meet your objectives.

. . . which will give you the . . . you want.

☐ *Action Step*

This is the specific closing step. This note says what needs to happen next for the buyer to get the value of your Idea. It should be as specific as possible and include who is to do what and when.

The Action Step frequently sounds like this:

The next step is your approval today.

All that's needed is your okay by Tuesday and we can start in May.

Going forward, I'll be seeing the research department on Friday. Can I tell them that you are in favor of this program?

To get started, just say yes and I'll set up the meeting with senior management today.

Let us return to our travel consultant, who is ready to conclude after giving an engaging, relevant, interesting, and compelling presentation. Figures 5-3, 5-4, and 5-5 show three versions of that closing summary. Become Alex, the buyer, again. In your role as Alex, which summary has the most selling power for you? Which summary is most satisfying? Which summary moves you along most easily to the Action Step? Which summary makes you feel most favorable toward the seller? Notice the notes.

You probably find Summary #1 (Figure 5-3) weak because it shows the novice at work. This summary, which is very self-serving, is totally unconnected to the buyer. It basically says, *I, the seller, think this is a good idea* ☼. *Hurry up and agree,* ☐ *so I can get on to my next appointment.* Why are we not surprised that a buyer might feel cornered, rather than comfortable, and say, *No-o-o, I don't think so?* The travel consultant is playing her own sales music so loudly

Figure 5-3. Travel consultant's summary #1.

Notes	Summary
☼	In summary, I think your group should come to Rocky Mountain Resort. It's fabulous.
☐	All I need from you is a letter of intent by Tuesday for the week of August 10. Can I pencil you in for those dates?

Figure 5-4. Travel consultant's summary #2.

Notes	Summary
💡	In summary, I think your group should come to Rocky Mountain Resort. It's a fabulous place, and . . .
☺	Your people will have a wonderful time!
☐	All I need is a letter of intent from you by Tuesday for the week of August 10. Can I pencil you in for those dates?

that she is causing the buyer to cover his ears to escape the noise, rather than wanting to buy.

You probably find Figure 5-4 a reasonably good summary. As the work of an average presenter, it's not bad. The seller's idea 💡 is at least connected to the buyer's objective ☺ (*Your people will have a great time*). Then comes the action step ☐, during which the buyer may, or may not, buy. The seller may hear, *Let me think it over*.

Summary #3 (Figure 5-5) shows your star presenter in full

Figure 5-5. Travel consultant's summary #3.

Notes	Summary
🙁	In summary, your people are used to first-class meetings where they can both work and play hard. This year, in particular, you want to do something special for them.
💡	As you've seen, RMR is a fabulous place. You'll score a home run with it because you get 1. the best amenities and activities 2. awesome scenery, and 3. guaranteed good weather
☺	In short, your people will have a wonderful time!
☐	The next step is simple. To hold August 10–15 for your group, all you need to do is send us a letter of intent by Tuesday. Shall I pencil you in for those dates?

swing. Loudly and clearly, she is reinforcing the beat with the buyer. She is saying, *I, the seller, have understood* your *interests, Mr. Buyer* ☺. *Let me make it easy for you to remember what we discussed what you'll be getting,* ♡ *and how it once again accomplishes your objective* ☺. Notice also how the Action Step ☐ is couched in less self-serving language by replacing the *I need* with *all you need to do is . . .*

The buyer in Summary #3 is much more likely to feel cared about, listened to, and drawn into, rather than pushed and shoved into, the Action Step. No wonder he also feels positive toward the seller!

Summary #3 is strong, not because there are more words in it, but because it has the right elements in it (hits the right notes) that create the strongest sense of completeness, or closure, for the buyer.

Warning: Don't Miss the "Magic Moment"

If you are rolling through your presentation with your buyer and he is liking what he is hearing, is making positive comments, and is giving you all kinds of buying interest indications (*Really! . . . That's terrific! . . . I didn't know that! . . . You mean we could get . . . This is wonderful! . . . When could we start?*), you don't want to say, *Hang on. I read this book and I have three steps to go through before we can move to the Action Step.*

Heck no! Jump to the Action Step! Your buyer is ready to buy!

Personal Jazz!

Once again, you'll see that you personally sound better when you hit the right notes in your summary than when you leave them out. Switch gears from being Alex, the buyer, and become the travel consultant, the seller, in each of the three examples above. *Say* each of the summaries as written, as if you were presenting RMR to a potential meeting planner buyer. If you want to slightly alter some of the phrasing to accommodate your style, that is fine. (*Hint:* Allow yourself to pause at the end of each step for emphasis and a dramatic touch.) Notice which summary gives you a natural conversational flow and easy rhythm or pace. Notice where you sound the most definitive, most in control, most confident, most authoritative, and most interested in the buyer. (Use the tape recorder to really hear the differences.)

Clearly, the third pattern once again gives you double duty presentation power. It increases your buyer's comfort level and likelihood of saying yes, and it strengthens your personal delivery skills as well.

Additional Examples of Jazz! Summaries

Summaries are relatively easy to play. Read and say out loud the summaries in Figures 5-6, 5-7, and 5-8 to give yourself a chance to *catch the sound* that you can use in future presentations to get clients to move comfortably to saying yes.

Figure 5-6. Formal summary (money managers to corporate pensions committee).

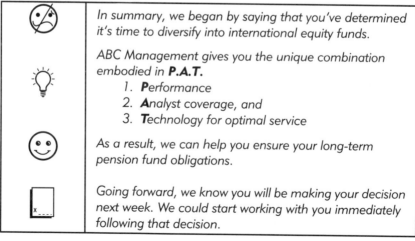

	In summary, we began by saying that you've determined it's time to diversify into international equity funds.
	*ABC Management gives you the unique combination embodied in **P.A.T.** 1. **P**erformance 2. **A**nalyst coverage, and 3. **T**echnology for optimal service*
	As a result, we can help you ensure your long-term pension fund obligations.
	Going forward, we know you will be making your decision next week. We could start working with you immediately following that decision.

Figure 5-7. Informal one-on-one summary (furniture systems rep to purchasing agent).

Okay, so let's see where we've been. Basically, your business is booming, which gets you to the bank a lot. However, that growth is playing havoc with your office space because you're locked into your existing lease for the next two years. So, the challenge is to maximize the existing space.

We've reviewed a number of options and our best recommendation is the Furniture Flex System.

1. It gives you maximum flexibility
2. It's ergonomically state-of-the-art for comfort
3. It provides an attractive environment in which to work

Bottom line, Sam, you'll be able to manage your space needs successfully no matter how much your business grows.

To get started, the first step is to allow us to come in and do a space-needs analysis. Can we set that up for next week, say Monday at 2 P.M.?

Figure 5-8. One-to-a-small-group summary (magazine ad sales rep to marketing executives at Sports Unlimited sportswear).

In summary, Sports Unlimited has a great product, but it's not top of mind with teens, your target market.

Teens Today is the perfect place to raise your visibility. Teens Today gets you a direct line to
- The most teens
- Who spend the most money on sportswear
- In the best environment to support your advertising

Bottom line, advertising in Teens Today will help increase your market share.

We can start the campaign with the next issue or select future special issues. What would you like to do?

The Jazz! Summary Format

The Jazz! summary format (Figure 5-9) is similar to, but not identical with, the introduction format. The icons and their definitions are on the left. The words in italics to the right of the icons are merely suggestive to give you a sense of the flow of the summary. Obviously, you have your own style and may alter the phrasing slightly to suit yourself. However, like the Jazz! introduction format, if you are strapped for time, you can use the phrases in italics and you'll never go wrong. Just fill in the blanks and you will have your buyer moving to the Action Step with you.

In the Spotlight: It's Your Turn

It's time to turn coach again to see how Jazz!y your summaries are. Return to the sample presentation that you selected in Chapters 1 and 3.

Figure 5-9. Elements of a Jazz! summary.

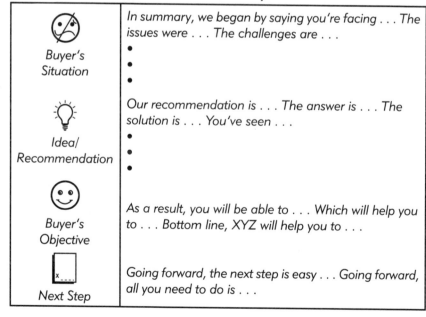

Just as you did with your introduction, you will "score" your summary on paper. Take a sheet of paper. Leave a margin of about an inch on the left side of the page. Write out in full, or in bullet points, what you would normally say in the summary of your presentation to a buyer. Starting each sentence on a new line will make it easier for you to label your summary with the notes.

Then, mark your presentation in the margin with any of the notes from Figure 5-2 that apply.

Now, tape yourself saying your summary. Play your summary back and listen to it as your buyer would hear it. How strong is its closing power?

Compare your summary pattern to the three patterns in Figure 5-10. Which pattern does your summary most resemble? Your answer reveals the kind of sales music you tend to play in the summaries of your presentations. This music is a good indicator of how easily you move buyers to say yes.

Figure 5-10. What kind of sales music are you playing?

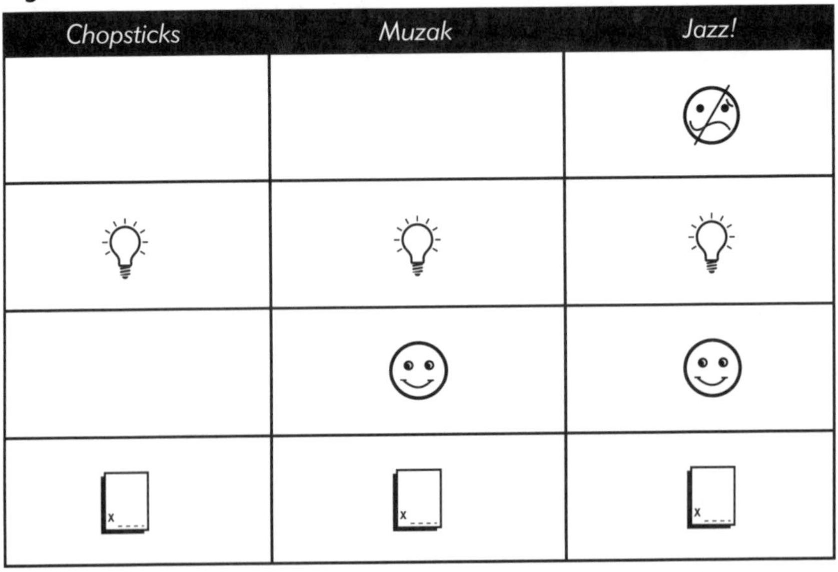

Chopsticks	Muzak	Jazz!
		☹
💡	💡	💡
	☺	☺
⬜	⬜	⬜

They're "Nodding Their Heads," but Is It Yes! or No!?

Answer the following questions to determine your specific areas of strength and weakness.

1. *Is there a* brief *recap of the Buyer's Situation?* 🖉
   Yes? Good. Your buyer appreciates your recognition of his original situation.

   No? You may appear more interested in your commission than sympathetic to your buyer's circumstances.

2. *Is there a brief re-cap of your Idea/Recommendation?* 💡
   Yes? This helps crystallize in your buyer's mind what you have said. He will feel as if he understood everything. He can retain it easily. If he has to repeat your Idea to a superior, a crisp recap means he will be able to do that easily.

   No? There's a good chance you will leave your buyer with only the most general sense of what he heard, which will often lead to a reaction of, *I'll have to think about it.* Or if your recap is very long, you will lose your buyer. Remember, if you haven't sold him on your ideas during the presentation, you're not going to do it by trying to repeat the entire presentation in the last ninety seconds of your summary.

   Tip: "Like perfume or cologne, less is better" in summaries as well as in introductions.

3. *Is there a link back to the Buyer's Objective?* 😊
   Yes? Getting their objectives fulfilled makes buyers happy and motivates them to act.

   No? By omitting this step, you're missing a very important psychological moment for your buyer. Buyers care more about getting what they want than they do about a seller's Idea.

4. *Is there a specific "who-what-when" action step?* ☐
   Yes? You're likely to get a positive response.

   No? Your meeting may end inconclusively. It's important for you to state the Action Step. You may have noticed that buyers don't tend to close themselves. If your presentation has been relevant, interesting, persuasive, involving, and easy to follow, this will be easy to do.

Polish Up Your Star!

By now, you know the routine. Rework your summary until you're satisfied it will move your buyer to action. If it's missing, add a brief reference to the Buyer's Situation. If it's long-winded, state your Recommendation crisply with up to three brief points to remember. Add in the link back to the Buyer's Objective if you omitted it. Check that next step to make sure it's specific and time-related. Tape yourself with your new summary and listen to the result.

Circle Still Not Quite Closed?

Summaries are fairly straightforward and most people find them easy to do. However, they have a few potential clinkers in them as well. See Chapter 6 to make sure sour notes are not sneaking into your summary.

Summary

 We began by saying that buyers need a real sense of closure at the end of a presentation to feel satisfied.

 The Jazz! Summary, with this sequential pattern from Figure 5-2, fills that need.

It is:

* Short
* Upbeat
* Powerful

☺ Playing these notes in your summary will result in a buyer who is ready and willing to move to the Action Step with you.

▢ Going forward, the Next Step is simple. Use the Jazz! summary format in the conclusion of your next presentation.

6

Clinkers

Common Mistakes in Summaries

**"Well, by golly, that was a real treat.
Now what are you selling?"**

You saw in the previous chapter that a summary is a short recap of a presentation and the prelude to moving the sale forward easily and naturally to an Action Step. The clinkers to guard against are:

Rambling

Rambling in the summary means the same as it did in Chapter 3, which is going beyond what is necessary. Rambling shatters any sense of finality and closure. Instead, your buyer wonders where you are going and if you will ever get there. See Figure 6-1.

Look at your summary. Can it be crisped up?

Total Replay

It is futile to try to stuff ten, fifteen, twenty, or even more minutes of a presentation into a one- or two-minute recap of your Idea/ Recommendation. It's like trying to fill a three-pound chicken with ten pounds of stuffing. It doesn't work. You can't do it. And when you do it in a presentation, you only confuse your buyer. It is more effective to use short, simple sentences. See Figure 6-2.

Obviously, if you want to leave buyers with four things in the Idea/Recommendation step, you can. However, the more things you leave buyers with, the more you threaten their sense of comfort, balance, and order.

Laundry lists of points to remember also tax the limits of a person's memory. Think what happens when you find yourself in a grocery or hardware store trying frantically to remember everything on a long shopping list that you left at home. The more items on it, the harder and more stressful it is to remember. If you insist on leaving buyers with a long list of selling points to remember, then group them into three categories.

Look at your summary. Have you made it easy for your buyer to remember the heart of your Idea/Recommendation?

I-Strain

This occurs when the focus in a summary is seller-centered, rather than buyer-centered. (See Figure 6-3.) A self-serving summary is

Figure 6-1. Rambling vs. Jazz!

Rambling		Jazz!
In summary, you have sixty people who love to play golf, and who have been going to southern resorts. They had a particularly challenging year and you want to reward them appropriately. You're looking at a number of alternative locations, for example, blah, blah, blah, blah.		In summary, you want the best place possible for your sales meeting.

very jarring and can generate mistrust for your buyer. Look at it this way: Do you like it when other people tell you what to do? How likely are you to do what they want? Buyers respond the same way. Instead of feeling comfortably closed, they will feel pressured.

Look at your summary. Is it buyer-centered?

The "Unfinished Symphony"

Many salespeople get all the way to the end of a very compelling presentation and then hit a real clinker: They don't close! They stop

Figure 6-2. Total replay vs. Jazz!

Total Replay		Jazz!
Well, you'll score a home run with Rocky Mountain Resort. Built by a businessperson for businesspeople thirty years ago, it has ten meeting rooms, all with views, a great restaurant with a renowned chef whose food is just fabulous, along with blah, blah, blah, blah.		You'll score a home run with Rocky Mountain Resort. You get majestic scenery, state-of-the-art facilities, and enough activities to satisfy everyone.

Figure 6-3. I-strain vs. Jazz!

I-strain		Jazz!
The next step is simple. **I need** you **to give me** a letter of intent by August.	[x....]	The next step is simple. Just sign this letter of intent to guarantee your August dates.

just short of the Action Step. By definition, the Action Step means your buyer agrees to *do* something at some definite time (for example, approve something; sign something; say yes to something; schedule something; or recommend something).

When you stop short of the Action Step, it's like preparing someone for a kiss, moving closer, puckering up, and then suddenly freezing. Don't disappoint your buyers. Complete the presentation to the Action Step. (See Figure 6-4.)

Look at your summary. Does it *kiss* your buyer or does it leave him or her with a sense of incompleteness?

Figure 6-4. The "unfinished symphony" vs. Jazz!

The "Unfinished Symphony"		Jazz!
Example #1		
As a result, we can help you increase market share. (Seller stops, smiles, and waits—and waits—for buyer to close.)	[x....]	As a result, we can help increase your market share. The first step is to set up a meeting with Pat. **Can we do that Thursday?** (Buyer) *Friday at 2 is better.* (Seller) *Fine, Friday at 2.*
Example #2		
So, that's it. What do you think? (Buyer) *Sounds good.* (Seller) *Good.*		So, that's it. What do you think? (Buyer) *Sounds good.* (Seller) **Great. Will you recommend us to Jack this week?** (Buyer) *Yes.*

Wrong Note

This clinker is about the appropriateness of the Action Step for a particular buyer. Imagine that a friend has asked to borrow $10 to buy something. You would probably say okay. Now suppose that friend wanted to borrow $10,000 to start a business. Chances are your answer would not be such an automatic yes. You might agree to look at the business plans. You might agree to test the widget the friend wanted to produce. You might agree to sit down with a lawyer and a banker to review the viability of this business. But it is unlikely that you would immediately agree to give this friend the $10,000.

The same is true in presentations. Make the Action Step *appropriate* to the circumstances and to the limits of the decision-making ability of that buyer. You want to make it easy for the buyer to say yes and move the sales process forward. (See Figure 6-5.)

Look at your summary. Is the Action Step appropriate for this buyer at this stage of the sales process?

Self-Assessment

Consider your summary again. Think of past presentations. Think of any feedback you may have gotten from colleagues, managers, or customers. Which clinkers might you be hitting?

Figure 6-5. Wrong note vs. Jazz!

Wrong Note	Jazz!
Jack, the next step is to allocate funds for this event. Will you sign this order for $2,000,000?	Jack, the next step is to allocate funds for this event. Would you review this proposal and then let's meet Monday to address any additional questions and finalize the details. Okay? (Buyer) *Fine. My office at 8:30.*

Clinker	Not a Problem	Needs Work	High-Priority
1. *Rambling* Saying more than is necessary	——	——	——
2. *Total Replay* Trying to repeat the whole presentation in a ninety-second recap	——	——	——
3. *I-Strain* Being too self-serving in the Action Step	——	——	——
4. *The "Unfinished Symphony"* Failing to close with a specific Action Step	——	——	——
5. *Wrong Note* Asking for more than your buyer can say yes to.	——	——	——

Jazz! Up Your Summary

Return to your summary. Use the results of your self-assessment to make any changes to it until you are comfortable that you are playing the sales music most likely to *move* your buyer to the desired Action Step.

"All right," you're saying. "I really see the advantages of looking at the selling power revealed in my presentation patterns, but one thing bothers me. Where does creativity come into play? A lot of the really terrific sales presenters are successful because they do ingenious things to make their points. I wish I could do that!"

You can. If the sales music up to this point has been "toe-tapping, head-nodding, smooth jazz," the next chapter gives you lots of ideas for stepping up your level of play to "Le Jazz Hot!"

7

Le Jazz Hot!

The Creative Touch

"I have an idea whose time has come
and I can't do anything about it."

Look at Figure 7-1. How many squares do you see? Now turn to Figure 7-21 at the very end of this chapter. Did you see that many initially?

Like your experience with the squares, there are always many creative opportunities possible in even the most technical sales presentation. You just need to *see* the opportunities and then decide which ones you want to include to Jazz! up your presentations.

Figure 7-1. Sixteen squares.

Where and When?

You can use creativity at any point in the presentation. The only limit on your creativity is your imagination. The only caveat is that wherever and whenever you take a creative leap, it has to be timed right, pitched at the right level of sophistication for your audience, and must make the point.

Expensive, flashing, multimedia megashows are not necessary, although they can certainly enhance a presentation. That type of presentation is the exception rather than the rule for most salespeople. At most, you may use a software graphics program to create a tailored laptop presentation. (We will talk about what constitutes effective visuals in Chapter 8.)

Instead, this chapter is about easy, no-to-low-cost ways to creatively capture a buyer's attention, keep him interested in your material, and move him to action. Creative touches include unusual openings and closings; painting pictures; stories, quotes, provocative questions, games or props; themes that run throughout a presentation; and cartoons.

Cartoons, like the ones in this book, are a low-tech way to make a presentation more interesting and entertaining. They can be used at any point in a presentation to capture interest, reinforce a point, or provide appropriate humor.

Creativity in Introductions

You can begin your presentation with a short, relevant story, props, a game, or a provocative question. Be careful of beginning with a joke, unless you have tested the joke on a business associate and you are absolutely certain it is relevant, in good taste, and that your timing is perfect. Here are several examples of creative introductions.

Use a Story

Ever since prehistoric times, people have loved stories. They work very well in presentations as long as they are short and relevant to the topic at hand. See Figure 7-2 for an example of a seller who uses an amusing story that relates directly to the buyer's situation.

The story in Figure 7-3 helped a seller save a client who was furious about a mistake her company had made with his business. She was asked to compete for additional business and to justify why her company should win it after their error.

Another salesperson used a story in an unusual way at the Idea Step in her introduction (see Figure 7-4). She was trying to convince a reluctant buyer to rent in an area that, although a bit run-down now, was expected to improve rapidly.

Figure 7-2. Using a story to open.

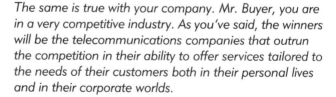

BACKGROUND:
Seller is selling sophisticated communications technology.

Seller: *Two boys go camping, and as they are turning in for the night, they hear noises in the woods. Sure enough, it's a bear. The first boy starts to run like the wind. He suddenly realizes his buddy isn't with him and when he looks back, he sees his friend frantically putting on his sneakers. "What are you doing putting on your sneakers?" shouts the first boy. "You'll never outrun the bear!" His friend yells back, "I don't have to outrun the bear; I just have to outrun you!"*

The same is true with your company. Mr. Buyer, you are in a very competitive industry. As you've said, the winners will be the telecommunications companies that outrun the competition in their ability to offer services tailored to the needs of their customers both in their personal lives and in their corporate worlds.

What's the best way to do that?

The answer is network intelligence and specifically XYZ Network Intelligence . . .

. . . which will help you increase your market share and revenues!

Figure 7-3. Using a story to save an account.

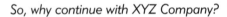

	Good morning. As I stand here before you, I am reminded of what Abraham Lincoln said when he was asked how he felt after he lost an election for Congress. "I feel like you do when you hit the funny bone in your elbow. I'm too old to cry, but it hurts too much to laugh." *That's a little bit how I feel this morning. I'm too old to cry, but the error our company made was too much to laugh about. However, like Abraham Lincoln, who continued to run for office in spite of that setback, I will continue to ask for your business because we can, indeed, help you meet your revenue goals for next year.*
	My understanding is you're facing . . . , *. . . , and . . . (Is that still correct? Buyer: Yes.)*
	So, why continue with XYZ Company?
	For three reasons. First, we have changed the procedures that led to the errors. Second, because you get . . . with us. And third, because. . . .
	These three factors combined will help meet your $50 million revenue target.
	I know you have concerns about past errors, so let's begin by looking at the procedures and safeguards XYZ has put in place to protect you from any recurrence. And since your success and our business relationship are very important to both of us, please ask any and all questions throughout this discussion.

What stories can you use to grab a buyer's attention in your introductions?

Use Props

Props are immediately engaging because they are visual and unexpected. They arouse the buyer's curiosity. This seller is able to use her props twice to good effect in the introduction in Figure 7-5.

Another salesperson who was selling training seminars placed

Figure 7-4. Using a story for your idea.

	Seller: Mr. Buyer, you're looking to increase business by opening more stores.
	You've told me you want a location that is heavily trafficked, at a reasonable rental, with upscale customers. You've seen the plans for location X, but you're concerned that the neighborhood isn't quite right.
	Buyer: Yes, I can't afford to make the wrong move. Seller: I hear you, so, why is this a good move? Let me ask you a question. Do you know who Willy Sutton was? Buyer: Wasn't he a bank robber? Seller: Yes! And when they caught Willy, they asked him why he robbed banks. Do you know what he said? Buyer: What?
	Seller: Because that's where the money is! Mr. Buyer, location X is where the money is! 1. It's the fastest growing neighborhood in the city. 2. Other top stores are already opening up there. 3. You can lock in a very favorable long-term lease now before it really takes off.
	Mr. Buyer, opening a store in location X will be like buying Microsoft stock in 1984*—a very good investment for your long-term growth. *Notice the analogy thrown in to emphasize the value of making this move

a wad of jumbo-sized dollar bills on her client's desk at the Idea/ Recommendation Step of her presentation to reinforce the point that her company could save this prospect a considerable amount of money ("big bucks") by using her company's services. She got the business.

What props would work in your introductions?

Play a Game

A game can be used to reflect a buyer's situation or to challenge him or her on a negative perception. A perception game draws

Figure 7-5. Using props to sell.

BACKGROUND	BACKGROUND: *Marketing company representative calling on a liquor account with sagging sales.*

	Seller begins her presentation by taking out three clear plastic cups into which she pours some of the buyer's liquor. She fills the first cup to the client's left three quarters full. She fills the middle cup half full. She fills the third cup one quarter full.
(frowning face)	*Greg, what's been happening to liquor sales at XYZ Liquor Company in the last three years has been a precipitous drop in sales. This has been due to changes in drinking preferences, changes in demographics, and the heightened health consciousness in this country.*
?	*How can we reverse this trend?* (As she says that, she reverses the positions of the first and third cups so that the three-quarters-full cup is the furthest on the right, representing future sales.)
(lightbulb)	*Our recommendation is that you implement a revitalized marketing program that includes Strategy A, Strategy B, and Strategy C.*
(smiley face)	*Doing this will help increase revenues.*

people in immediately because it's challenging, fun, and drives toward the point your presentation will make. The example in Figure 7-6 is a game used to reflect the buyer's situation.

The sixteen squares exercise at the beginning of this chapter is a game that challenges you and plays with your perceptions. In preparing the opening to this chapter, I had two goals. First, I wanted to creatively model the theme of this chapter. Second, I knew whichever technique I selected had to lead to my Idea/Recommendation: Creative possibilities exist and salespeople *can* be creative if they just *see* those possibilities. I also know that many salespeople think their job is to sell and that being creative is what

Figure 7-6. Using games to sell.

> *BACKGROUND:*
> Sales rep for a consulting company is calling on a human resources executive in a recently downsized company who has internal credibility problems with the different divisions.

Salesperson draws the following:

and asks buyer what he "sees." Buyer replies, *The letter H, a goalpost, the Hilton Hotel logo, a neck and necklace, etc.*

Seller: *How about two people trying to get the same seat on a train!* (That is usually followed by a small chuckle from the buyer.)

Seller: *Why did I do this with you? Because this is what's happening now in your company. Because of old management history, people in the company have only one perception of your department and it's a poor one, as you've said. But you know there is another way of seeing your group and you'd like the rest of the firm to see them in a fresh light.*

Now, how do we change the firm's perceptions?

One proven way is to take advantage of our unique internal staff marketing program . . .

. . . which will help your department to be seen as the true added value it is.

their marketing and promotion people do. I wanted to change that perception. However, before I could get you to change your mind, I had to get you to open it! The sixteen squares exercise, when used at the beginning of a presentation, is the perfect "mind-opener."

When done with a group of buyers, the sixteen squares exercise is particularly effective. People will compete with each other stating, with absolute certainty, that there are only seventeen, twenty-one, or whatever other number of squares they think they see. Then, when you show them all the possibilities and use the lesson of the game to lead them to your Idea/Recommendation, you have their undivided attention. (*Warning:* Be prepared for the answer "an infinite number." That is possible, if you look at the squares in three dimensions. If that happens, agree quickly. It still proves your point that there are more possibilities in the sixteen squares than most people originally thought.)

Suppose you have a buyer who believes that your company is too small to handle the volume of his business. You could open your presentation in the manner shown in Figure 7-7.

Use a Startling Fact and/or Question

Giving presentations on financial or technical topics can be very daunting. However, Figure 7-8 shows an example of how a seller

Figure 7-7. Using another game.

Seller: *Mr. Buyer, let me ask you a question. What do these beliefs clearly have in common?*
- The world is flat.
- Women shouldn't have the vote.
- Man will never fly.
- The Berlin Wall will never come down.

Buyer: *Obviously, they were all at one time taken as gospel and all were eventually proved wrong.*

Seller: *Yes. And there's one more belief that you'll find equally wrong: XYZ Company is too small to handle your company's work! What I'd like to show you today is how we can not only handle your work but do it to exceed your expectations.*

Figure 7-8. Making a dry topic interesting.

	BACKGROUND: *You are a financial planner selling to a group of small business owners.*
	Flash (or show) a few newspaper articles on a screen that predict that by the year 2010 we will need some astronomical number of dollars in order to live at the same standard of living we enjoy today.
	Ask. (In a large group, raise your hand as you ask) *How many of you have seen these articles recently in the financial press?* (Many people will nod. In a large group, many will raise their hands.)
	How many of you have retirement plans that will allow you to save this much money for your retirement? (Fewer nods and fewer hands.)
⊘	*Not surprising* (you say). *Most busy business people have little time left over at the end of the day to plan for their future. But that can cost you and your family a great deal.*
?	*What are the kinds of things you should be doing?*
💡	*Basically, there are three things you need to do . . .* A. xxx B. xxx C. xxx
😊	*The result will be to ensure that you have a comfortable retirement.*

used a question to interest her buyers immediately on a financial topic.

In Figure 7-9, a career change counselor wanted to sell the idea that anyone seeking a job had to explore many avenues simultaneously: friends, libraries, books, advertisements, old business contacts, etc. To drive home this point, she opened her presentation with several questions.

Figure 7-9. Opening the presentation with questions.

	Good morning. Let me ask you a question. If someone you loved (a child, parent, spouse, or friend) was diagnosed with a terminal disease, had only a year to live, and you were told there was a doctor in this country who could save that person, how many of you would find that doctor? Raise your hand. (Everyone raises their hands.) Next question. How would you find this doctor? (They shout out a variety of answers: Call friends, go to their own doctor, check out university libraries, go on the Internet, write to congressional representatives, etc.) Good. Last question. Would you do these things one at a time and wait for a response from each before making the next contact, or would you do all these things simultaneously? (Simultaneously, they all answer.) Exactly. Your goal to find that doctor is too important to waste time or to leave any stone unturned. What does that have to do with career change? The process you just described is exactly the process you need to find your next job: Do research and develop multiple, simultaneous avenues of contact. That type of networking and activity will help you meet your employment objectives. Let's start to compile the kinds of contacts you can make . . .

How can you use provocative questions to creatively open up your presentation?

Creativity in the Middle of Your Presentation

Similar techniques are effective in the middle of your presentations as well. In the example in Figure 7-10, the seller addressed an objection using props. She realized that the essence of her buyer's

Figure 7-10. Addressing an objection.

Advertising sales representative is selling a series of advertisements to a client who wants to test one advertisement, review the number of responses it pulls, and then run additional advertising space, but only if the first advertisement pulls well. This is a strategy that the seller knows is wrong.

Seller brought a hammer, a block of wood, and a nail on the call and asked the client to pound the nail once into a piece of wood. Afterward, she asked her client to pull the nail out, which he did easily.

She then asked the client to pound the nail into the wood six times. When she asked him to pull it out this time, he was unable to.

Exactly, she said. *Like the nail in the wood, Mr. Buyer, it doesn't pay to hammer home your message only once. If you want your message to take hold in the minds of readers, you must repeat it with frequency.*

objection had to do with his misunderstanding as to how advertising frequency (running advertisements more than once) affects results. She came up with the clever solution in the Figure.

In one case, at a large publication where this idea was used, the advertiser jumped to a six-time contract from the original one-time commitment. At another, smaller publication, a buyer went from a commitment of $400 to $24,000. In both cases, the sales representatives received a huge return on their investment in an inexpensive hammer, block of wood, and nail. All it took was a little creative thinking.

The seller mentioned earlier who used the "big bucks" example in her introduction could just as easily use it in the middle of the presentation. She could give away some of the big bucks to her buyer when she got to the cost/benefit page in her presentation. Alternatively, she could give different amounts of the big bucks away on every page of the middle of the presentation with every selling point. For example, if she is describing the content of the seminars, she could translate the value of the increased skills learned to a dollar figure—and give out a "big buck." When she shows her list of other satisfied clients, she can give out several big bucks, as she indicates how much value the training added to these companies. At the end of the presentation, the buyer would be sitting with lots of big bucks supporting the seller's Idea that working with her company is a good investment.

What buyer objections or key selling points lend themselves to using props in your presentations?

Use a Quotation

A familiar quotation, saying, or proverb with a ring of truth to it and/or a famous person behind it can help you drive a point home as well. An example of a quotation that is both true and said by a well-known entertainer is in Figure 7-11.

This seller is using a common proverb to encourage a buyer to look at his product.

What relevant quotations, proverbs, or sayings can you weave into your presentation to make your point?

Use Comparisons (Analogies and Metaphors)

We discussed the power of analogies and metaphors in Chapter 3. They are highlighted here again because they are a very powerful and creative way to increase your power of persuasion and to help people understand complex information.

A sales trader was explaining a new and somewhat complex

Figure 7-11. Using famous quotations to sell.

  	Seller: *Mr. Buyer, Will Rogers once said, "Even if you're on the right track, if you just sit there, you're going to get hit!"* *Right now, Mr. Buyer, you are relatively satisfied with your current supplier, but with all the changes in technology and with the increased competition you mentioned earlier, can you really afford to continue to do things the same way?* *Look at the many advantages you would get with our company servicing your account . . .*

investment instrument with an unwieldy name, Tax Exempt Equity Investment Fund. Essentially, an investor would put money into the fund, leave it there for a specified number of years while it presumably increased in value, and then, when the time was up, the investor would get his money back with appreciation.

Her challenge was to make this unwieldy sounding investment simple to understand and memorable to her buyers. Her solution was to look outside her immediate world of investments and trading for parallel situations in other worlds or fields. She was seeking something she could compare the fund to that would make it easy to understand. Common worlds from which to draw analogies are sports, politics, nature, life, theater, or worlds known to a buyer, such as family, golf, tennis, travel, the buyer's industry, or cities.

Our seller's thought process went something like this: *I want people to quickly and easily grasp the concept behind this fund. I need a situation where you put something away for a while, it increases in value, and, at the end, you get the reward. Let's see. In sports, you invest time in spring training and then a few months later, you've got a winning team. No, I don't like that comparison. In theater, you bring all the elements of a play together, spend time in rehearsal, and then at showtime, you open on Broadway, hopefully, with a hit. No, that's not quite it either. In the world of nature, what is there? I've got it! Caterpillars and butterflies! Caterpillars cocoon for a period of time and then emerge as beautiful butterflies. That's perfect.*

She compared the fund to a butterfly, explained that the investor's money "cocoons" for a period of time, during which it grows in value, until ultimately the investor winds up with a "butterfly," an appreciated asset.

In her presentation, the seller referred to the financial vehicle as the "Butterfly Fund" and explained its meaning.

The butterfly analogy transformed what could have been a very dry, easily forgettable topic into an interesting, and easily understood, presentation. As an extra touch, she had a butterfly logo for the fund on her visuals. Her presentation went very well.

In the case in Figure 7-12, an insurance agent was trying to show her client the wisdom of buying life insurance sooner rather

Figure 7-12. Instilling wisdom in the buy.

Seller: *Mr. Buyer, you like these trees, don't you?*
Buyer: *I certainly do! They give me great pleasure.*
Seller: *What would happen if you didn't take care of them?*
Buyer: *Well, they wouldn't do very well.*
Seller: *They sure wouldn't. Did you ever think that your family is like these trees?*
Buyer: *What do you mean?*
Seller: *Well, if you weren't here to care for them, they wouldn't do so well either, would they?*
Buyer: *You've got a point.* (He smiles sheepishly.) *I guess I should stop procrastinating about that insurance.*
Seller: *I guess so.*

than later in his life. The client, who had a family, didn't want to deal with it and kept coming up with reasons to delay the purchase. The planner also knew that the client loved taking care of some apple trees that were on his property. Finally, the planner went to visit her client one Sunday, when she knew the client would be tending to his trees. After initial small talk, the conversation took this turn.

Comparisons (analogies and metaphors) are creative uses of language to make points clear and instantly understood. What analogies or metaphors can you use to drive your points home or make your information easier to understand?

Play on a Theme Throughout the Presentation

When you know of a buyer's interest or hobby, you can use it as a running theme throughout the presentation. Buyers are amused, flattered, and, more important, stay interested in your information when you do this.

In the example in Figure 7-13, the advertising sales representative for XYZ magazine was not getting business from a buyer who thought his customers did not read her magazine. In her presentation, she decided to capitalize on her prospect's known love of bowling to win him over.

Figure 7-13. Capitalizing on a prospect's interest.

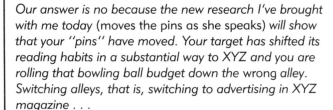

	Seller: Mr. Buyer, this bowling ball is your media budget, the pins are your target market and the alley is Competitive Magazine B. You've been rolling your media budget down the same magazine alley for the last ten years to hit your target market. Buyer (smugly): Right, and we're very happy with that plan.
	Seller: Yes, it has worked well for you in the past, but the question is, Will it work as well for you in the future?
	Our answer is no because the new research I've brought with me today (moves the pins as she speaks) will show that your "pins" have moved. Your target has shifted its reading habits in a substantial way to XYZ and you are rolling that bowling ball budget down the wrong alley. Switching alleys, that is, switching to advertising in XYZ magazine . . .
🙂	. . . will help you increase your business more effectively in the future.

She began by taking out a miniature bowling ball and pins, which she then set up.

The supporting information in the middle of the presentation played on the bowling theme. The visuals had headers such as "Strike with XYZ!" The summary had a bowling score sheet showing the client winning with XYZ.

Corny? To you and to me, perhaps, but not to this buyer who loved bowling and wound up giving this magazine his business.

What opportunities exist for you to theme a presentation to an interest of one of your key prospects?

Paint Pictures

When a good travel agent sells a particular vacation, she doesn't just say, *Go biking in France. It's a beautiful place.* Instead, she'll paint a picture of what biking in France will be like for you. For example, she might make a presentation such as that in Figure 7-14.

Figure 7-14. Painting pictures.

> *Each morning, you wake up to the aroma of fresh coffee and sit down to breakfast in a fairy tale-like, five-hundred-year-old chateau. After a delicious croissant with jam, you begin a day of glorious cycling. As you ride back roads through the countryside, you are the only person in sight. You look out at fields of six-foot-high sunflowers waving in the breeze under a crystal clear blue sky. You stop in small villages and sit outdoors sipping local wines and eating pates and cheeses that would cost a small fortune back home. Then, . . .*

With descriptions like this, you're probably thinking, Where do I sign up?

Whether you sell consulting services, computers, or construction equipment, paint a picture for your buyer of what it will be like to use your product or services. For example, see Figure 7-15.

How many different ways can you paint pictures for your prospects and clients to give them a feeling and a picture for what it will be like to use your product or service?

Creativity in Your Summary

If you opened with a story or other attention-grabber, return to it in your summary. For example, suppose you had used the earlier bear story in your introduction. Your summary might look like Figure 7-16.

Quotations, sayings, or proverbs also add a creative touch in a summary. In Figure 7-17, the seller uses a saying to create motivation and urgency for taking the next step.

Figure 7-15. Painting more pictures.

> *This system will really transform your workday. You'll be free to work on the special projects you mentioned earlier. You'll get your reports out on time. You'll be able to route them any way you wish. You won't have to stay until 8:00 P.M. every night. Instead, you can be home with your family or out with friends. Also, . . .*

Figure 7-16. Summary using the bear story.

	In summary, you've said that the key to your growth is the ability to offer a variety of tailored and low-cost personal and corporate services to your clients.
	With ABC Intelligent Networks, you get the sneakers to outrun your competition. You get: • the latest technology • quality service • a unique partnering system that guarantees a smooth operation
	All of which means continued and expanding growth for you in the twenty-first century.
	The next step is to try on the sneakers. Let's set up a meeting between our senior associates and your tech team later this month.

Figure 7-17. Using a saying to create motivation and urgency.

	In summary, you want . . .
	ABC can solve that for you. You'll get . . . , . . . , and . . .
	Which will increase your department's productivity by 20 to 25 percent.
	In terms of next steps, you know what they say, Mr. Buyer, You can't steal second base without taking your foot off first. So, if it works for your calendar, let's get started on phase one on Wednesday.

In Figure 7-18, the seller from XYZ Employee Benefits Company uses a widely reported remark from a well-known and respected entertainment figure to emphasize the positive value the buyer will realize when he agrees to move forward with the seller's recommendation.

What quotes, proverbs, or sayings would be effective and appropriate to use in the summaries of some of your presentations?

Figure 7-18. Using a celebrity remark to emphasize positive value.

	In summary, Mr. Buyer, your employees have been asking for a new benefits plan for years.

	The new features we recommend will give your employees and your company:
	  • xxx
	  • xxx
	  • xxx

	In terms of your employees' reaction to these changes, they'll feel like Steven Spielberg when he won the 1993 Oscar for best director for Schindler's List, *after being passed over for the award for several years. He said, "This is the best drink of water after the longest drought in my life!" Your employees will feel the same appreciation when you add these new features.*
	Shall we go ahead this week and draw up a final proposal to include these changes?

(A list of some quotations you might want to use appears at the end of this chapter.)

Le Jazz Hot! Benefits

Creativity transforms star presenters into superstar presenters. Creativity:

- Distinguishes you from your competition.
- Makes your selling points with greater impact.
- Makes it easier to win the business!

Creative Idea Sources

Where do you find these stories, quotes, and ideas? Stories, quotes, and analogies abound in newspapers, business magazines, airline magazines, and book collections of business and life quotations. For example, as this book was being written, *The Wall Street Journal* ran a news item about the Justice Department questioning Microsoft Corporation's right to add yet another feature to its Windows™ operating system. The article quoted Bill Gates attacking the Justice Department's case by saying: "The 1995 consent decree explicitly allows the company to keep integrating functions into the operating system. For the Justice Department to get in the middle of that process *would be like the government in 1932 deciding that cars shouldn't have radios because that would hurt the radio makers.*"

In the November 10, 1997, issue of *Fortune,* an article on a planned luxury cruise ship, which will sell onboard condominium apartments, communicated the opulence of this ship by saying, "It is, without a doubt, the ne plus ultra in cruising. *Resident Sea is to Carnival and the Love Boat what Buckingham Palace is to home.*"

In an October 29, 1997, *New York Times* essay, "The Non-Panic of '97," William Safire made the point that the 550-point drop in the stock market two days earlier was not, in fact, the big drop that some people feared. To drive the point home, he wrote, "Like Californians after a mild quake, we can say, 'But this wasn't the Big One.' "

Although I have seen the following story in a number of publications, I first read it in an airline guide years ago. It's about a college experiment involving a frog and boiling water. It can be used very powerfully in a presentation to create a sense of urgency in your buyer to act now, rather than later.

Ask your buyer to guess what a frog does when it is thrown into a pot of boiling water. Your buyer will answer either that the frog jumps out or that he doesn't know what would happen. If he answers the former, say *Absolutely right!* If your buyer doesn't know, tell him what happens. Then say, *But do you know what happens when you put a frog in a pot of cool water and turn the heat on?* Most people will say they don't know. And you say, *He dies, because by the time he realizes he is in trouble, it's too late. He is too weak to jump out. Mr. Buyer, by your own admission, given the challenges you described to me earlier, your company is "in the pan of water and the flame is on." Don't let it get too late. Jump out now. Invest in . . . product to start cutting your costs today.* Pretty powerful. If you use this story, be certain it is appropriate to the situation and to the individual buyer.

Whether you use the frog story or not, the point is that stories, analogies, examples, startling facts, and numbers are all around you in your normal reading. Be on the lookout for them, let them stimulate your thinking, and use any that fit your business.

For truly dramatic touches, like the hammer, nail, and wood example, get into the comparison thinking habit. Ask yourself what you can compare your point to, or use, to make a point that your buyer will understand. Let your mind free-associate to all kinds of parallel situations taken from sports; raising kids; manufacturing; the economy; team dynamics; or any world, field, or thing that you know will be familiar to your buyer. Do that until you hit the one idea that will work. If nothing comes to you, ask a friend or colleague to brainstorm ideas with you. When we work on creative ways to present ideas and handle objections in my seminars, salespeople, who think they are not intrinsically creative, are amazed at how many ideas they can produce quickly when they work with one or two other people.

Build Your Analogy Thinking Power

Below are several easy exercises to help you jump-start your comparison thinking power. Do them by yourself or with colleagues at a weekly sales meeting. You'll be amazed at how many ideas are produced.

1. In everyday conversation, make yourself use comparisons. If you are relating a story, talking to a colleague, or making a point with your child, get into the habit of saying, *It's just like* . . .

2. See how many connections you can make between your product or service and any of the following: a color, a celebrity, a sport, a city, a song, a car, a holiday, an animal, or a store.

3. Most products and services have processes or procedures involved in their implementation. For example, in money management, there is an investment selection process; in education, there is a teaching process; in manufacturing, there are many processes.
   - What is the process in your business?
   - What can you compare that process to in order to help your buyer more easily understand how it works?

       Is your process like one-step shopping? Like the checkout system in the supermarket? Like applying for college? Like island hopping on a vacation? Like a snake shedding its skin? How?

4. How is life like a roller coaster, an orchestra, or a toothbrush? List as many parallels as possible for each one.
5. How are kids like a computer? a meal, a river, or a flashlight? List as many parallels as possible for each one.

Just as physical exercise strengthens your muscles, these mental exercises will strengthen your creative thinking muscle as well.

Self-Assessment

Replay your presentation in your mind. Recall other presentations to other clients in various situations. Think of feedback you have received from managers, colleagues, and customers. Look at Figure 7-19. Into which category do you currently fall?

ARE YOU PLAYING LE JAZZ *HOT!* OR LE JAZZ LUKEWARM?

1. *Do you try to be creative with every presentation?*
   Yes? You keep your information lively and fresh for buyers. They probably look forward to seeing and working with you.

       No? Over time, you become predictable to buyers. You make it easy for them to feel like they know your product or service and don't really need to see you again.

Figure 7-19. What kind of creative music are you playing?

CHOPSTICKS (Novice)	MUZAK (Average)	JAZZ! (Star/Superstar)
No creativity	Occasionally creative	Frequently creative
Occasional analogies	Tends to use the same techniques and/or analogies over and over again	Tailors analogies to each buyer Uses a variety of creative techniques
Uncomfortable with offbeat techniques	Doesn't mind being creative, but doesn't put much effort into it	Always on the lookout for fresh ideas, stories, and techniques

   2. Do you use analogies and examples specifically tailored to each buyer?
       Yes? Buyers are more inclined to feel comfortable with you.
           No? You may come across as canned. On a personal note, you may find yourself bored with your own presentation, and that feeling likely gets communicated to your buyer as well.
   3. Do you vary your use of creative techniques?
       Yes? You probably appear more spontaneous and interesting than other salespeople.
           No? Again, you may come across as canned.

Polish Up Your Star!

Review your presentation. Look for places where you can Jazz! it up with some creative touches (stories, games, props, provocative questions, quotes, proverbs, sayings, a theme, or cartoons). Tape yourself. Play the tape back. See what you think of the result.

Clinkers

Can you hit sour notes while being creative? Unfortunately, yes. See if you are unintentionally hitting either of these creativity clinkers.

Wrong Notes

Your buyer will cringe with embarrassment, boredom, or annoyance if your creativity technique is inappropriate or endlessly long. It's like the person who thinks it's clever and witty to run around a party with a lampshade on his head. He may have done that with great success at a fraternity party in college, but he failed to recognize that what worked in one place does not work in a different environment.

I once witnessed a woman using several quotations throughout her presentation to make various points. They were really strong quotes. The only trouble was that they were all sports quotes said by Vince Lombardi, the famous football coach. She was talking to a group that was 100 percent female, most of whom were not raving football fans. Great quotes. Wrong group.

Always try your ideas on a colleague first before you spring them on clients.

Missing a Beat

This happens when what you do or say fails to connect to the point you are making. You must link the story, question, prop, quote, or cartoon to the point you are making. See Figure 7-20.

Recall your presentations. If you are hitting any of these clinkers, think what you need to add, eliminate, or modify to get back on key, creatively speaking.

Summary

1. Creativity, whether in sports, business, or music, gives magic and more meaning to a performance. It transports listeners from the mundane to higher levels of understanding, involvement, and pleasure.
2. Sales stars and superstars selectively use the following creative touches in their presentations to create that kind of

Figure 7-20. Missing a beat vs. Jazz!

Missing a Beat	Jazz!
(seller cuts up a $100 bill and says)	
You wouldn't waste $100 this way. That's why you need a new system . . .	You wouldn't waste $100 this way. *Yet every time your people process an approval form, they are in effect wasting as much as $100 per form, because of the old system you are using. The way to recover your losses is to . . .*
This product is like an octopus.	This product is like an octopus. *It can handle up to eight jobs simultaneously.*

    magic in their selling:

stories	quotations	themes
provocative questions	props	analogies
analogies	games	cartoons

3. Creative touches need to meet three criteria:
   A. They should be appropriate to your buyers
   B. They need to be timed right
   C. You must clearly connect them to the point you are making
4. Play Le Jazz Hot! and . . .
   - You'll make your information more memorable for your buyer.
   - You'll be more appealing personally as a sales professional.
   - You'll sell business more easily.
   - You'll have more fun in the process!

Useful Quotations, Proverbs, and Sayings

The following sample list of quotations, proverbs, and sayings is one that I have used over the years, or have saved to use in the future. I found them in my general reading and in various collections. It's a good idea to keep a file of ones that you like, so that they are easily available to you when you need them for a particular sales presentation.

1. *For buyers who are fearful of change:*

   "If you think you can, or, if you think you can't, you're probably right."

   —Henry Ford

   "A man flattened by an opponent can get up again. A man flattened by conformity stays down for good."

   —Tom Watson, Jr.

2. *For buyers who are willing to sacrifice quality for price:*

   "Once you say you're going to settle for second, that's what happens to you in life, I find."

   —John F. Kennedy

3. *For buyers who could improve their productivity with your product:*

   "It is not enough to be busy; so are the ants. The question is: What are we busy about?"

   —Henry David Thoreau

4. *For buyers who think everything is fine as is:*

   "Good enough never is."

   —Debbi Fields, Mrs. Fields, Inc.

5. *For buyers who are concerned about the time and effort it will take to make some change:*

   "When you win, nothing hurts."

   —Joe Namath

"I do not know how to get to the top without hard work. That is the recipe. It will not always get you to the top, but should get you pretty near."

—Margaret Thatcher

"The harder I work, the luckier I get."

—Sam Goldwyn, Lee Trevino, Thomas Jefferson, et al.

"The way I see it, if you want the rainbow, you gotta put up with the rain."

—Dolly Parton

"Everything comes to him who hustles while he waits."

—Thomas Edison

"You miss 100 percent of the shots you never take."

—Wayne Gretzky

6. *For a buyer who is hoping things will change all by themselves, or to create a sense of urgency to act in buyers:*

"One stands for long time with open mouth before roast duck fly in."

—Chinese proverb

"Even if you're on the right track, if you just sit there, you're going to get hit."

—Will Rogers

". . . as one goes through life one learns that if you don't paddle your own canoe, you don't move."

—Katharine Hepburn

7. *For a buyer who has suddenly found himself in a difficult situation:*

"When the world gives you lemons, make lemonade!"

—anonymous

8. *Miscellaneous quotes that I have always liked:*

"Nobody can make you feel inferior without your consent."

—Eleanor Roosevelt

"Never, never, never, never, never give up!"

—Winston Churchill

"Nothing great was ever accomplished without enthusiasm."

—Ralph Waldo Emerson

"A smile is the shortest distance between two people."

—Victor Borge

"Life is an adventure, or it's nothing."

—Helen Keller

"If you never fail, you aren't taking enough risks."

—anonymous

"The difference between ordinary and extraordinary is that little 'extra.' "

—anonymous

"Aerodynamically, the bumble bee shouldn't be able to fly, but the bumblebee doesn't know it, so it goes on flying anyway."

—Mary Kay Ash

"It's what you learn after you know it all that counts."

—anonymous

Figure 7-21. Thirty squares.

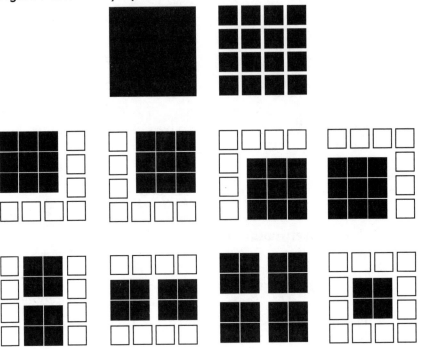

8

"See" the Music

Tips on Creating and Working With Visual Aids

Have you ever bumped into a person you know but can't place? What typically went through your mind as you tried to recall who the person was? Words? Numbers? Or pictures? *(I see grass . . . blue sky . . . you're small . . . I've got it! We were both at Camp Walla Walla, twenty years ago!)*

The fact is most people remember visually. In other words, we literally *get the picture.* In addition to buyers retaining more of what you are saying with visuals, good visuals also get your points across more easily. Even Einstein said, "If I can't 'see' it, I don't understand it."

When visuals are used, you are more persuasive, you can cover more ground in less time, retention and comprehension are greater, and your presentation is more interesting and involving.

If you are not using any actual visual aids, it becomes even more critical that you use lots of Word Pictures, such as examples, analogies, stories, testimonials, and numbers put into concrete terms. These create pictures in buyers' minds and help them *see,* understand, and retain what you are saying more easily.

Whether your visual aids are high-tech (electronic), low-tech (slides, overheads, flip charts, desktop flips, or books), or no-tech (handouts or samples), they need to support the sales music of your message. You don't want buyers tuning out because of boring or confusing visuals.

The Right Moment

Do you use a presentation at every meeting? When you do use a presentation, at what point do you take it out? The answer should depend on where you are in the sales cycle and what is appropriate to a specific situation.

If it's a first call on a client, chances are that most of the initial discussion will be about the client's objectives and business situation. If you sell complex business solutions (management consulting, systems, insurance, engineering designs, etc.), you may just want to talk in generalities about what your company does. You may spontaneously sketch out a rough diagram of a model or a process on a piece of paper, show a client list for credibility, or a piece of interesting research to whet your buyer's appetite, and then suggest a second meeting to more formally present a specific, tailored solution or idea for that client. On the other hand, if you sell a business product, such as office furniture, carpeting, or paper, then you will probably want to show your visuals (samples or pictures) in that same meeting, once you know what your buyer is looking for.

If you are at the second meeting, you would most likely take out the prepared, tailored presentation and go through it with your buyer after initial amenities.

The Right Visual Format

From single-page handouts to laptops to multimedia extravaganzas, you have many visual aid options. Your choice should be tailored to the situation. What follows is a general summary of the pros and cons of the different types of formats. The choice of format will also depend on your client. What is most appropriate? A sales presentation to a corporate board is probably better done with slides, overheads, or a computer rather than with flip charts. A sales presentation to a group of educators could use overheads or flip charts. In all cases, you may also choose to mix your formats, for example, overheads for the core presentation, a flip chart for spontaneous interaction, and a video to show examples.

For the latest in presentation technology, such as projectors, graphics software, laser printers, and other gadgets and gizmos, subscribe to *Presentations Magazine,* a monthly magazine published by Lakewood Publications in Minneapolis, Minnesota (1-800-328-4329). It is packed with the latest information on electronic presentations and sprinkled with articles on presentation tips. Another source for tools and advice on effective electronic presentations is provided free on the World Wide Web by Proxima Corporation, a leading producer of multimedia products (http://www.presenters university.com).

Flip Charts

Flip charts can be very effective for groups of no larger than seventy-five if people are sitting at tables or auditorium style. Flip charts are low-tech and inexpensive. Color is easily added with magic markers.

The downside is that if you are going to a client's office, you either have to bring previously prepared flips, or you must request that the client provide a flip chart and easel, and you will need to arrive early to prepare your visuals. After a while, previously prepared flip charts become frayed and can look unprofessional.

However, having a flip chart available to you in the room is very valuable, even if you are using another visual medium, like an overhead. You can turn to a blank flip-chart page and spontaneously work through a problem with your client, show how a process works, or develop a list of concerns, issues, or ideas. Just remember to bring your own markers.

Desktop Books or Flips

These are good with one or two people at most. They are portable and can be tailored to your buyers by changing the pages or the order of the presentation pages.

The danger is that you will fall into the trap of giving a canned presentation, that you will simply become a page-turner and reader. Avoid saying, ". . . and the next page shows . . . and the next page shows . . ."

Overhead Transparencies

These are effective with groups as large as three hundred people. They are easy to use and easy to add to or change. Most overheads can be used with the room lights left on. They take up little space when you travel, and most clients will have an overhead projector for you to use.

You can also achieve many interesting effects with them. You can use overlays, where one transparency is laid over another to dramatically show the result of a change. For example, your first transparency may show a line chart of the stock market's performance from 1987 to 1997. Then, your overlay would add the line of your company's performance to that chart in that same time period to show how much better someone would have done investing with your company.

You can use reveals. Suppose you sell design services. You can use a reveal to dramatically present the differences in a "before and after" picture of an office you designed. When you put the transparency on the projector, do it with a blank piece of paper *under* the transparency, covering up the right half of the page so that only the "before" picture shows. Putting the paper under the transparency keeps it from flying off the projector and also allows you, but not the audience, to see what is going to be revealed. Then, when you are ready to show the "after" picture, simply slide the blank piece of paper out from under the transparency. The effect on your buyer will be dramatic. You can reveal a list of items on a transparency the same way, moving the blank page down from top to bottom, one item at a time.

Warning: Don't overuse this technique. It should be used only when you are trying to create a dramatic effect or when you have a strong reason for covering up a list of items.

The problem with transparencies used to be that light from the projector would seep out from the sides of your visual. That problem has been solved with the invention of flip-frames, or acetate "sleeves" into which you slip your overhead. Flip-frames come with attached floppy panels that open up to cover a specific area of a projector. You can put notes on these panels for yourself. Another wonderful feature is that they are also three-hole punched, so they fit easily into a looseleaf binder, which makes them very convenient for filing and traveling. Flip-frames are available in any office supply store.

Tip: If you use overheads regularly, always carry an extra bulb with you. At the very least, identify how you switch bulbs on your projector, should the first bulb die in the middle of your presentation.

Test the overhead projector before you begin. Make sure it's in focus and that the lamp-head is up so that the image will project onto a screen. Instead of putting up one of your visuals for the focus test, thereby showing it prematurely, place your pen or a rubber band on the machine and focus with that.

Slides

Slides work well for large groups of any size. They project color brilliantly, look very professional, and are easy to travel with. They also show photographs to advantage. The downsides are:

1. They are very formal, which may not be the mood you want to create for a particular presentation.
2. You cannot easily move from slide #8 to slide #18.
3. Lights need to be dimmed.
4. They can be expensive to update.
5. They are dependent on a good slide projector that works properly and doesn't jam.

Tip: Make sure you load your slide tray properly and that you test the projector with your slides before the presentation. Remember that slides are placed in a slide tray differently for front view projectors and back-of-the-room projectors. If you are using slides, you will probably be working with a remote. Be sure you know how to use it.

Videos

Videos can be very effective if you set them up properly. Prior to showing a video clip, give buyers a task to do as they are watching it. Otherwise, they may just go to sleep for a few minutes. Instead of saying, *Take a look at how the plant operates on this video* or *Listen to what our customers have to say about product X,* try saying, *As you look at how our new plant operates, see how many advantages it has over your current operation* or *In listening to our customers, notice which of their situations are similar to yours.*
   Play the video. Your first question after it is finished becomes,

So, what advantages appealed to you? or *Which of their situations were similar to yours?* or (raise your hand as you ask this) *How many of you recognized your own situations in this video?* (Hands will go up.) Taking their answers, or using their raised hands as a response, gets buyers much more involved in the presentation than they would be otherwise.

Electronic Presentations

Laptop computers are good for presenting to one person. Because of its small screen size, it's hard for more than one person to see a laptop presentation. However, laptop presentations have lots of advantages. They are easily controlled and easily changed. They can create all kinds of interesting effects, including attractive color graphics, blow-ins, fade-outs, animation, sound, and video. You can also use them to work out problems, work with client specifications, and do computations right on the spot during the presentation. Laptops connected to a projector can do all of the above for any size group.

The downsides are the limitations created by your comfort level using the technology and the industry you are in. For example, if you are selling to the office supply industry, you may not need the bells and whistles of a computer presentation; samples and pictures may be sufficient. However, if you are selling to the high-tech industry, they expect to see electronic presentations.

Warning: If you are doing a computer presentation for a group, be prepared for every possible logistics disaster. Bring extra cables and an extension cord. Finally, bring an overhead version of the computer presentation. If your software fails, which it does more often than you would like, or if the equipment fails, you will be glad that you did.

Electronic Excess

The same principles described in this chapter apply to electronic presentations. Presentation programs like PowerPoint, Lotus Free-lance Graphics, Aldus Persuasion, and Astound, coupled with

LCD panels and modern projectors, are marvelous tools and work together to make presentations come alive with color, pictures, sound, video, and a variety of effects. However, they are only tools: *You* are still the creator and presenter of your message. No matter how many blow-ins, builds, or fades you can produce with your computer, if buyers are confused or bored by what they are seeing, you will have struck a bad visual chord with them. Don't go overboard with the technology. Keep it simple. You're there to make a sale, not to win an Academy Award for special effects.

Hitting the Right (Visual) Notes

There are a few simple guidelines for effective visuals, regardless of whether they appear on an overhead, on a desktop, or on a computer.

1. Good visuals are clear and simple, have few words, and are easy to grasp. A good rule of thumb for bullets is a maximum of six lines and no more than five to six words per line.

2. The best visuals are presented as bullet points, graphs, charts, or pictures.

3. Each visual should make only one point.

4. The best ones use color to attract, highlight, contrast, or create a feeling or mood.

- Red is exciting and "pops" on a visual.
- Green is a warm, comforting color (the color of money!).
- Blue is authoritative and is easy on the eyes as a background color.
- Yellow is a good contrast on a colored background, but will not show up on a clear background.
- Clear xeroxes of a printed page are very weak visual aids.

5. Props and the products themselves are obviously strong visuals as well. (See Chapter 7: Le Jazz Hot! The Creative Touch.)

6. Neatness counts. Check overheads for smudges, visuals for misspellings, and handouts or reports for frayed edges. If you are writing on flip charts, write large and clearly (blue-lined flip-chart pads help enormously for this purpose).

7. Remember that *you* are a visual as well. Good grooming, appropriate dress (no clanky jewelry, no extreme fashion, no excessive makeup), life in the eyes, and a smile on your face are the most important visuals in your presentation.

Controlling the Buyer's Eye and Ear

If you have a series of bullet points to discuss on a single page, and wish to discuss them one at a time, consider doing a build. Show the first. Talk about it. On the next visual, drop the first bullet back in tone and show the second in the prominent color. On the next visual, drop the first two back in tone and show the third in full color. You can do this with diagrams as well, showing the first part, then the second, and so on.

Match Your Information to the Right Visual

If you have to present straight text, use bullet points with as few words as possible per bullet. Compare the visual impact of the two examples in Figures 8-1 and 8-2. (Using Greek letters allows you to see the positive or negative visual impact on a viewer in a totally objective way.)

Is there a trend you want to show? Use line or area graphs. (See Figure 8-3.)

Are there relationships you want to bring out? Use pie charts. (See Figures 8-4 and 8-5.)

Do you want to compare different quantities or variables? Use bar graphs. (See Figures 8-6 and 8-7.)

Do you want to show categories and activities or criteria arranged in an organized way? Use tables or diagrams. (See Figures 8-8 and 8-9.)

Figure 8-1. Confusing bullets.

ΣΡΦΓ ϑΠΟ ΙΔΦΔΓϑ

- Μφκλκλ κγγγ φοιφ ξν
  Ργφδφ κφ μδφΥκδφφ δφ
  Οφλκλκγγγ φοιφ λν
- Μκλκλκ γγγ φοιφ σν
  Ω φκλκ λ κγγγ φοιφ ξν
  Λφκλκλκ γγγ φοιφ μν
- Δφκ λκλ κδγ φοιφ ων
  Αφκ λκλκγλγ φοιφ ον

Do you want to show a timetable or a process flow? Use a chart. (See Figure 8-10.)

The Power of Pictures

Add pictures or cartoons to any of the previous examples and you draw your buyer into your information even more. Think of the business visuals that appear in *USA Today* every day. They use hard data to create a business chart or graph, but they always include a single, strong pictorial element. Nearly all business publications

Figure 8-2. Clear bullets.

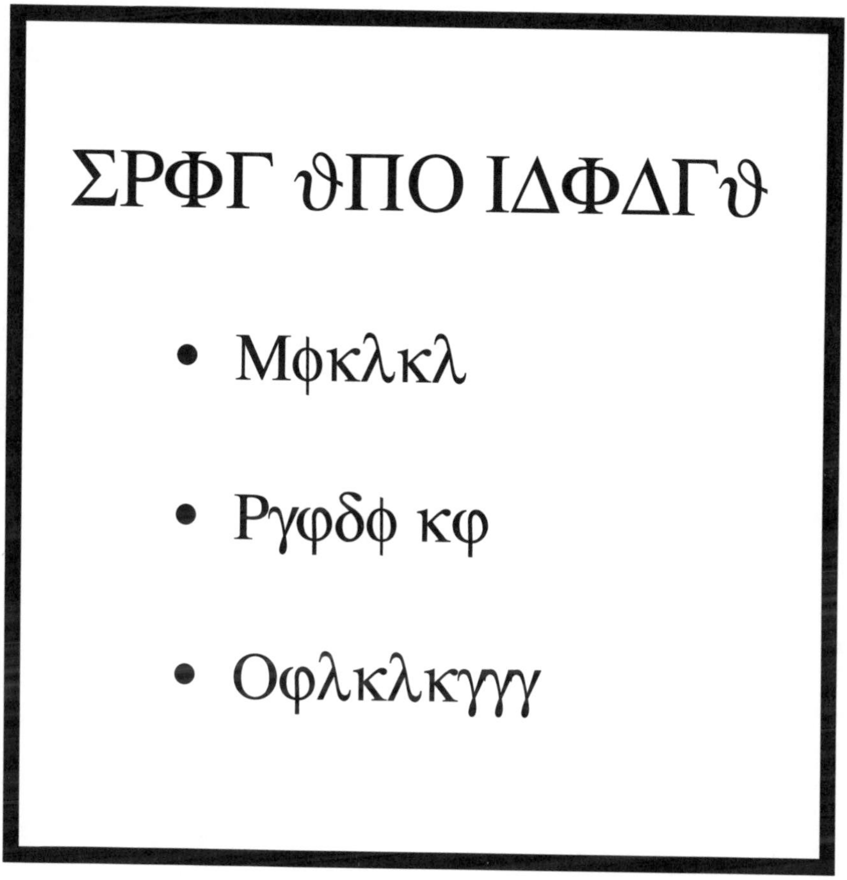

ΣΡΦΓ ϑΠΟ ΙΔΦΔΓϑ

- Μφκλκλ

- Ργφδφ κφ

- Οφλκλκγγ

do that. They don't do it to be cute, but rather because they know the pictorial element makes the information more appealing and easier to grasp by readers. (See Figures 8-11 and 8-12.)

In a boardroom situation, you may not want to use cartoons, but you can make your visuals attractive with color and appropriate logos or pictures. For example, in a presentation to the investment community, a tanker company showed pictures of tankers in various sizes to reinforce their data that the state of the world tanker market was shrinking.

Figure 8-3. Line graph.

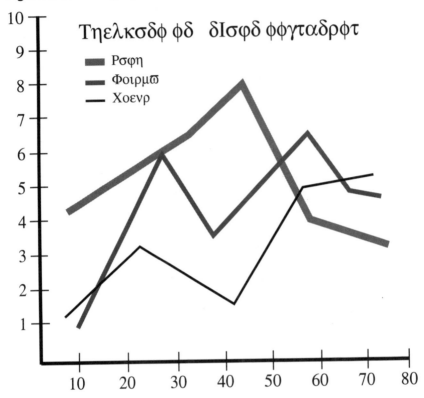

"Clear" Charts

When you present a graph or chart, tell people what they are look-ing at *before* you interpret the information. Don't show your chart or graph and say, *As you can see . . .* and begin to explain something in the visual. While you are merrily explaining the point, your buyer is still trying to figure out what he is looking at and, worse, he isn't really listening. To make sure you are both in sync with each other, *clear your visuals.*

For example,

1. You've just exposed a graph of sales results.
Say: *We compared sales results on the vertical axis with the dates of*

Figure 8-4. Pie chart.

ΤΗΕϑ ΦςΑΟΙΔΛ ΓΦϑΡΟΙϑΓ ΔΚϑ ΚϑΤ

■ ΣΟΧΙΑΛ ΣΕΧΥΡΙΤΨ

☐ ΕΑΡΝΙΝΓΣ

■ ΑΣΣΕΤΣ

■ ΠΡΙςΑΤΕ

■ ΓΟςΕΡΝΜΕΝΤ

■ ΟΤΗΕΡ

Figure 8-5. Three-dimensional pie chart.

Μεμβερσ βψ Γραδε

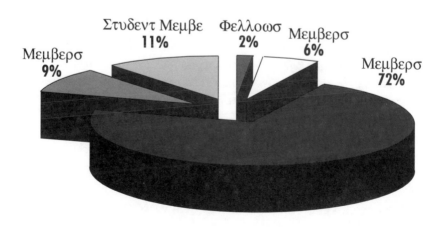

Figure 8-6. Bar graph.

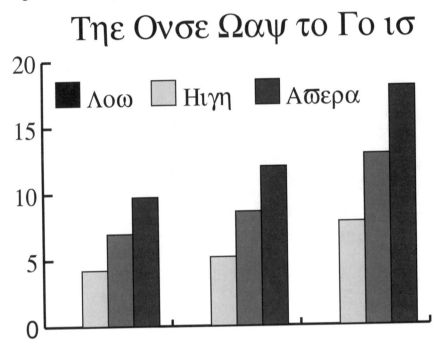

the direct mail drops on the horizontal axis. As you can see, the correlation is very, very strong.

2. You've just exposed a multicolumned chart that details potential savings.

Say: *The potential for savings is very high. Down the left-hand side of this chart we list each of your departments. Across the top of each column are the design features each requested. The costs of the features for each department are noted in the grid and the totals for each are in the last column. The differences are quite striking. For example, . . .*

Personal (Visual) Jazz!

What works for your buyer visually will improve your delivery skills as well. When a visual is text heavy, it forces you to look at

Figure 8-7. Bar graph.

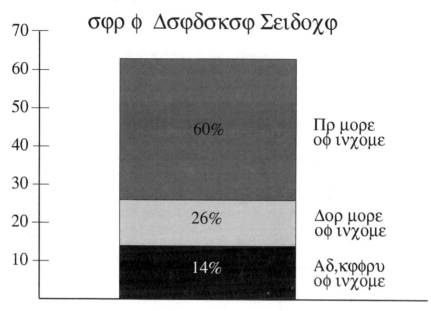

the screen, or at your notes, and read to the audience. Your presentation rapidly deteriorates into remedial reading and is a guaranteed formula for disaster. You will lose eye contact with your buyers, sound robotic, and become boring.

However, when your visuals are done effectively, they become the true aids they are meant to be. They will allow you to talk in a conversational, natural way, since *you* have to supply the context and content for the visual.

In the Spotlight: Your Turn

Look at the visuals you are using, or would use, in the real-world presentation that you have been working on in this guide. Use the grid in Figure 8-13 to determine how effective they are and how well you tend to work with them.

Figure 8-8. Diagram.

Δο ψOυ υνδερ ΣTαντ Ωηατ Tηισ Δαψσ

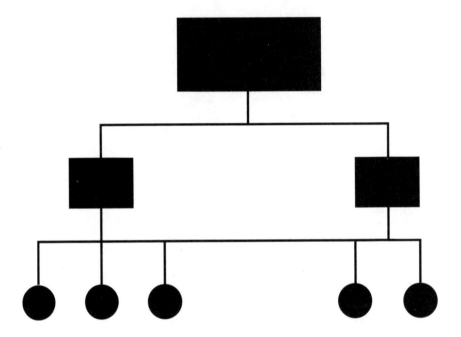

ANALYZE THE SELLING POWER OF YOUR VISUALS

1. *Are your visuals clear, big, simple, graphic, colorful?*
   Yes? You make it easy for your buyers to get your points.
      No? You risk buyers tuning out your message.
2. *Do you use a variety of visual types (bullets, graphs, pictures, etc.)?*
   Yes? You are likely to be more interesting, memorable, and persuasive.
      No? The same type of visual seen over and over again is as boring as a series of text pages and can make your message predictable and forgettable.
      Exception: If your main message, or story, is that you are number one in your field, then a series of bar charts showing you to be number one against every industry standard could be an effective use of the repetitive graphic.
      However, if all you are doing is using bullet points by default

Figure 8-9. Table.

Τυδωα	Εδισα	Τελι	Ωατδ	Σατι	Πριδ
ΜοινσΨ	✔	✔		✔	
ΡΥΩΑΣΨ		✔	✔		✔
ΩΘεδ	✔	✔			
Τηυρδαψ			✔	✔	✔
Φριδσαψ	✔	✔	✔		
Σατ	✔	✔	✔	✔	✔
Συνδαψ	✔		✔		

on each exhibit, then you are being visually lazy and your buyers will become bored.

3. *Are your eyes more on your buyers or more on your visuals?*
Eyes more on buyers? You are likely to be more convincing, animated, and persuasive. Eyes more on visuals? Buyers could leave the room and you wouldn't know it!

Tip: For group presentations, when you are standing at a screen, stand with your feet pointed more toward the audience than toward the screen. In this way, you can look at the screen, capture your thought, and your body and eyes will naturally want to swing to the audience, rather than stay on the screen.

Polish Up Your Star!

Review your visuals and revise them with the suggestions in this chapter, so that your visuals work for your buyer. Then go

Figure 8-10. Time flow chart.

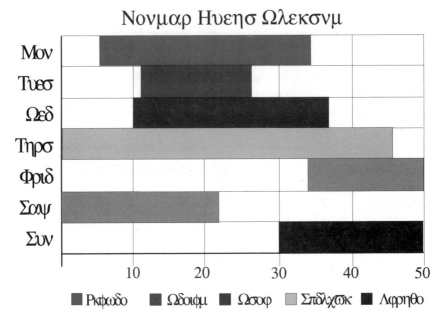

Νονμαρ Ηυεησ Ωλεκσνμ

Figure 8-11. Pictures and data.

Τηε Ονσε Ωαψ το Γο ισ

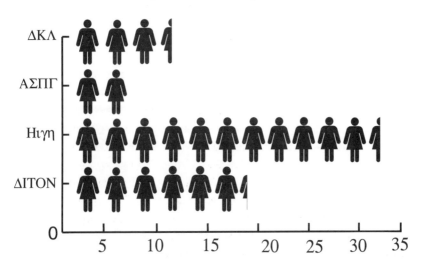

Figure 8-12. Pictures and concept.

Ρσδκλ Γφ φκΔΡΟπ

through your presentation again. It should be much easier to present.

Clinkers

There are two groups of potential clinkers to be concerned about. The first has to do with the visuals themselves. The second has to do with how you work with the visuals. Review the following list to see if you are inadvertently hitting these wrong visual notes.

Visual Overkill

There is such a thing as too much of a good thing. If a visual doesn't illustrate, explain, or support a point, get rid of it. Sometimes, the best visual is no visual! A page in a leave-behind copy of your presentation that might say *introduction* or *summary* has no business being shown on a screen in the actual presentation. A transition like *How does ABC Company do this?* is more effective when spoken than shown. The exception would be your title page, which is most effective when it has the client's objective, name, and logo on it, along with your company name.

Figure 8-13. What visual music are you playing?

Chopsticks	Muzak	Jazz!
Wordy visuals Busy visuals	Visuals clear, big, simple, graphic, colorful	Visuals clear, big, simple, graphic, colorful
	Sometimes wordy	Few words
	One concept to a visual	One concept to a visual
Occasional chart	Uses many visuals	Uses many visuals
	Uses too many of the same type (e.g., all bullets)	Uses a variety of visual types
Uses little color	Uses color	Uses color
Talks to visuals	Talks to visuals	Talks to buyers

"Horse" Charts

In Dallas, a participant in a GTE seminar said he hated "horse" charts. *What's that?* we all asked. *A horse chart,* he said, *is when you show a picture of a horse and title it "Horse."* Right he was! Let your headers be key buyer points, not just descriptive titles of the visual. Titles tell. Key buyer points sell! Compare the headlines in Figure 8-14.

Visual Fog

Suppose you are presenting drawings for redesigning a communications system. They could be fairly complex. A buyer looking at the whole system doesn't know what's important and what isn't. Use color to distinguish either different sections of the system or different pathways through the system. If you don't have color capability, use cross-hatching or shading to make the distinctions.

A second option is to use overlays or builds. If you are using

Figure 8-14. Headers as key buyer points.

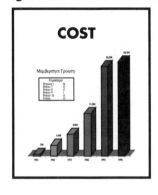

VS.

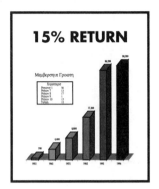

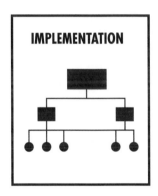

VS.

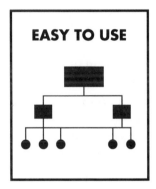

overheads, a third option is to work with a colored pen and circle or underline the relevant areas of the diagram as you talk about them.

If you are using simple handouts, either before or during your presentation, use a yellow highlighter or a red pen to highlight key points or numbers.

Remember, the eye is attracted to color. (That's why products are packaged in bright colors and advertisers are willing to pay a premium for four-color advertising in publications.) Use color to make the potentially meaningless meaningful for your buyer.

Blinding People

Do not begin your presentation with a blinding flash of light from an overhead projector. The flash of light hurts people's eyes. Always put your visual on the projector first. Then, turn the machine on. Follow the same procedure if you turn the machine off during the presentation to have a discussion with the group and then return to the projector to continue with the next visual. Place the visual on the machine before turning it back on. However, it is not necessary to turn the machine on and off for each overhead during the flow of the presentation.

Talking to a Machine

Always give your key points looking at your audience, not down at the projector or at your remote for the computer.

Pointing

If you are using your hand to point to something on a screen, use the hand that is closest to the screen. It allows you to easily point and still talk to the audience. Avoid crossing your body with the outside arm, because doing that will cause you to turn and talk to the screen.

If you are using a pointer, touch the part of the visual you are explaining. Don't let your hand jump around with the pointer on the screen. You will confuse people or cast many distracting shadows on the screen. The same is true with a laser pointer.

Never point at people with either your finger or a pointer. You will remind them of every negative authority figure in their lives from a scolding parent to an angry teacher or resented boss. Instead, use the neutral gesture of pointing with a full, open palm.

When You Don't Want to Be in the Spotlight

Avoid getting caught between the projector light and your screen. You risk momentarily blinding yourself from the projector light and you look a little foolish wearing your visual on your face and body.

Unexpected Mayhem

Your slides are coming up backwards. Your overhead projector bulb blows. The extension cord you need from the projector to the nearest outlet is missing. The cable to connect your computer to the projector is gone. Your videotape is coming out garbled on the monitor. You left your key handouts on your desk.

The Boy Scout motto applies: Be prepared. I said this earlier in the chapter, but it bears repeating. Carry extra cables, markers, bulbs, and handouts with you. Bring a three-prong conversion plug for two-prong outlets. If you are doing a very important computer presentation, have a backup set of overheads and an overhead projector readily available in case you run into software or computer difficulties. These computer presentation glitches happen more often than you would expect.

Always carry your visuals with you. Otherwise, you can wind up in Portland, Maine, while your visuals find themselves with your luggage in Portland, Oregon.

Get to your meeting early and check out all the logistics. For large meetings, get the name, in advance, of the on-site audiovisual specialist who can help in a real emergency and call her before the meeting to double-check everything.

Whatever medium you are using, from simple flyers to sophisticated multimedia extravaganzas, preparation, rehearsal, checklists, and back-up are critical to ensure that your sales music plays successfully.

A Necessary Visual Aids Lifesaver

Always bring your sense of humor with you in these mishaps.

A salesperson whose slides became hopelessly jammed during a presentation said, *Well, when you get lemons, make lemonade!* She then proceeded to describe the remaining slides with her hands. *Imagine the following graph. On the vertical axis, you have . . . On the horizontal axis, you have. . . . The trend line moved like this* (and using the total space in front of the room, she used her hands in very large gestures to make her points). Bottom line, she salvaged what could have been a disaster.

Think about how you work with visual aids and correct any of the above clinkers to strengthen your visual selling power.

Summary

1. Retention, persuasion, understanding, and interest are greatly increased for your buyers when visuals are used.
2. The purpose of a strong visual aid is to explain, illustrate, or support a point.
3. Visuals are most effective when they are big, simple, have color, use few words, and, instead of a descriptive title, have a selling key buyer point as the headline.

See Figure 8-15.

After going through these first eight chapters, it is clear that selling power in a presentation does not happen by accident but by design. In the next chapter, we'll review the kind of planning you'll want to do to maximize that power.

Figure 8-15. Best visuals.

Bullet Points

ΣΡΦΓ ϑΠΟ ΙΔΦΔΓϑ

- Μφκλκλ

- Ργφδφ κφ

- Οφλκλκγγ

Graphs

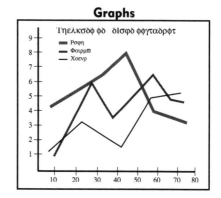

Charts

Pictures

9

Think Through the "Tune"

Planning

"Please hold my calls. I'm calibrating my sights."

Musicians do it. Chief executives do it. The best sales presenters do it as well. They plan before they perform. In a Jazz! presentation that means:

1. Planning the presentation's dynamics.
2. Developing a strong selling story.
3. Shaping the presentation to suit your buyer's style.

In this chapter, we'll focus on number one, planning the presentation's dynamics. Numbers two and three will be handled in Chapters 10 and 11.

When There's No Time to Plan

Imagine a fairly common sales situation. You are at an initial meeting with a prospect. You introduce yourself. You and the prospect exchange appropriate small talk before the conversation turns to his business. There are some questions about your company, but most of the meeting is a normal information gathering discussion about his business. He talks about his objectives, his business, his needs or specs, his timing, the decision-making process, his budget, his past experience, the other options he is considering, and any other key information associated with his business. Then, he asks you to tell him how your company can help him. He wants to know about your capabilities, your experience, your competitive advantages, costs, etc. In fact, this information is so important to him, he decides to call in a few of his colleagues to hear what you have to say.

Do you panic?

Absolutely not. Performing on the spot is analogous to what jazz musicians do when they improvise on their instruments: They build on their technical know-how and create music right in the moment. Like them, you will be able to build on your technical presentation know-how with Jazz! to create the right sales music for any given client.

In those on-the-spot sales presentations, recall the basic Jazz!

icons and framework and use them in combination with what your buyer told you to prompt the organization, or flow, of your presentation. The more you use the icons, the more automatic they become. It becomes easier and easier to spontaneously begin a presentation, to make your information interesting and persuasive, and to summarize to a natural close. As we said at the beginning of this book, it's like learning a piece of music. After some practice, you know the melody and can play the notes without looking.

If necessary, you can use the starter phrases you've seen in this book to move you through these presentations on short notice. For example, assume the buyer and seller in the situation in Figure 9-1 have just completed a discussion about the buyer's business and the buyer has said, *Okay, Ms. Seller, so tell me now what you think you can do for me.* You can see how a salesperson who knows the Jazz! "melody" could give a reasonably good on-the-spot presentation.

An impromptu Jazz! presentation may not be as creative as it would be if you had more time to think about it, but it will still be music to a buyer's ears: engaging, relevant, meaningful, and persuasive.

When There *Is* Time to Plan

In other situations, you do have time to prepare. You've had initial meetings with clients and they've asked you to come back with your best ideas or recommendations. Now you have the luxury of being able to think through everything about the presentation—from the tone you want to set to the information you want to include to whom else you want to bring, etc.

The easiest way to plan a presentation is in stages. In stage one, you determine the basic dynamics of the presentation (who, what, when, where, how long). In stage two, you block out the presentation in broad terms to make sure it contains the right things in the right order. In stage three, you add refinements, the additions that will Jazz! up the presentation and transform the basics into a persuasive, interesting, compelling, winning presenta-

Figure 9-1. Basic Jazz!

(Introduction)	
☺	Love to. Let's just recap to be sure we didn't leave anything out. You said your goal is to . . . and
✍	The situation is . . .
?	Is that right? (Buyer: Yes) Okay, so why does it make sense to work with us?
☼	Basically, because we can offer you A. . . . , B. . . . , and C. . . .
☺	Which will help you to . . .
›	Here's how we do that . . .
(Middle)	
📁	First, we can . . .
!	which will give you . . .
🗔	For example, . . .
↻	How does that sound?
›	Next, we also . . .
🗔	For example . . .
🗔	It's like . . .
!	Bottom line, you get . . .
↻	Do you see how that could work for you?
›	Another benefit is . . .
(Summary)	
	So, to sum up, Mr. Buyer,
✍	You're facing . . .
☼	With my company, you will get A. . . . , B. . . . , and C. . . .
☺	Which will help you to . . .
🗒	The next step would be to . . . Can we do that on . . . ?

tion. In stage four, you review it to make sure it's as Jazz!y as you want it. Planning in stages will save you more time than if you tried to think through everything at once.

Stage One

Use the questions in Figure 9-2 to think through the basics for a winning presentation quickly and efficiently. They cover your interests, your buyer and the buyer's world, your content and visuals, and other relevant considerations.

Stage Two

In stage two, block out the presentation to give yourself a bird's-eye view of the entire thing. If you are using a presentation graphics program, you can do this on your computer. Otherwise, use 5- by 7-inch index cards and lay them out in sequence on a table, or on the floor, as in Figure 9-3. Leave a half-inch margin down one side of each card. You will use this space after you're finished to check how strong your presentation really is. (You can also print out your computer presentation and lay those pages on the floor or table to give you a larger overview of the entire presentation.)

For purposes of having a complete walk-through of your presentation, have cards for every step of it, even if you do not intend to have an actual visual for that step. For example, have a card for the Setup Question in your introduction, even though you do not intend to have an actual visual for it. Draw rough sketches on the pages where you expect to have actual visuals.

Walk through the entire presentation to be sure the order is right: that there is a correct introduction, that you've included all the important information you need in the middle, and that there is a strong summary. Review how you will transition from card to card and where your buyer would benefit from hearing a mini-summary. Rearrange the cards until you are satisfied that the order and flow are correct.

Figure 9-2. Answer these questions.

My Interests

1. What is my objective?

2.   A. How do I want my buyer to feel at the end of the presentation?

   B. What specific Action Step (☐) will the buyer have to take to demonstrate that my objective was met and that he feels good about working with my company?

3. How much time will I have for the presentation? For questions?

My Buyer and My Buyer's World

4. Who is my buyer?
(Position? Level of sophistication about my product/service?
What do I know about my buyer's hobbies, interests, background, prior jobs? Tendency to be aggressive, cautious? Preference for details? Big picture? Bottom line?)

5. What tone or mood is appropriate for this buyer?
(Casual, businesslike, light, exciting?)

6. What is my buyer's business picture?
   A. Buyer's Objective? (☺)

(continues)

Figure 9-2. (Continued)

B. Buyer's Business Situation (🖉)

What's up? good?	What's down? bad? under pressure? a need?
◆	◆
◆	◆
◆	◆

The Content and Visuals

7. *Based on the answers in 5, in as few words as possible, what is my idea/recommendation?* (💡)

8. A. *After they hear my Idea/Recommendation, what questions will they have?*
(What is it? How does it work? How much time? How does it compare to my other options? What does it cost? What's your experience?)

B. *What is the best Information (data, facts, explanations, research) to provide to answer these questions?* 🗂

C. *What Key Buyer Points do I want to make with this Information?* ❗

9. *What visual aids, if any, will I use with this Information?*

Other Considerations

10. A. *What questions, doubts, and objections will my buyer have?*
(Jargon that needs to be defined, politics, personal credibility, past bad experience, buyer's close relationship with competitor?)

B. *Do I want to address these in the presentation or wait for them to come up as questions?*

C. *If I am going to address these in the presentation, what is the best way to do that?*
(Bring my manager? Get special research? Invite buyer to visit our plant or call a satisfied client? Bring special information? Be prepared to do a demonstration?)

11. *Who else from my organization should be on this call?*
(A technical/financial/research person? My manager?)

Figure 9-3. Block it out.

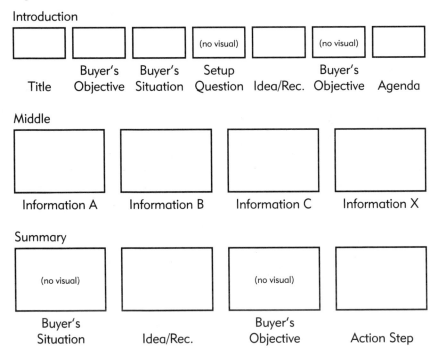

Stage Three: Jazz! It Up

Information in bullet points, graphs, charts, and/or pictures on the cards is what you will ultimately show your buyer. However, you know that information by itself, however accurate, falls flat with buyers unless there are other elements presented along with it to make it relevant and interesting. In stage three you add those elements.

Look at the cards you've laid out in the middle of your presentation. Now practice what you intend to say with each of those Information cards. You want to be certain your buyer finds everything you are saying relevant to his world. To ensure that, ask yourself, What is the Key Buyer Point (KBP) I want each Information card to make for my buyer? You may also have other secondary benefits or conclusions on a single page. Sometimes, you may have one piece of Information that runs to two or three cards (for example, how your product or service works). However, when you finish the three cards, the question still is, What is the major key benefit or conclusion you want that person to draw from the Information?

Then, decide if you want that KBP to be *written out* as the header on your visual, or do you simply want to *state* the KBP at the beginning or end (or in both places) of that Information? For example, if you are showing how an investment process works, do you want a descriptive title for the header and will you say the Key Buyer Point, or do you want a Key Buyer Point for the header itself? Do you want **A** or **B**?

A.	**B.**
Investment Process Explain diagram	**Maximize Return With** **Lowest Risk** Explain diagram

(spoken) *This approach maximizes your return with the lowest possible risk.*

(option) *Restate KBP*

If the explanation of your Information takes a while, it's a good idea to repeat the KBP for your buyer at the end of it.

There is no right answer. It's your judgment call, but the important Jazz! point here is that somewhere, either written or spoken, there needs to be a Key Buyer Point for *all* your Information *to make it relevant to the buyer.*

Next, make your Information both interesting and easy to understand for your buyer. Review the Information cards and decide where you will inject appropriate Word Pictures ⌨ to make your Information come alive for the buyer (examples, stories, analogies, testimonials, quotations, or numbers translated into concrete terms).

Look for Information that will be hard for your buyer to understand or hard for your buyer to accept. The best way to overcome those hurdles is to use an analogy. For example, a consultant was making a recommendation to a chief executive officer of a major company based on research he had done on the CEO's company. He explained the results of the research with a diagram. The CEO didn't understand it. He explained it again. Still, the CEO didn't get it. There was no point in explaining it yet a third time. So, the presenter reached for an analogy and said, *Sir, think of this data on your company that you're looking at as a snapshot. All you're seeing is what your company looked like frozen in that moment in time.* Bingo. Understanding what a snapshot is, the CEO immediately understood how to interpret the information he was seeing.

An analogy won the business for another salesperson when all the odds were stacked against her. An advertising agency was looking for presentation skills training. They sent out requests for proposals (RFPs) to every major presentation skills training company in the city and had as their first buying requirement that whoever they hired would absolutely have to have had other advertising agency clients. Our presentation skills salesperson did not meet that requirement. She knew that to simply list her credentials in other industries, however impressive, would not work. She needed to neutralize their perception that previous agency experience was important.

It took her three days to find just the right analogy to do that. She reviewed everything she knew about the agency, the people, their business, and their accounts. One known fact was that the agency had just won a new account in the cosmetics industry. Let's call the account Beauty, Inc. Using this information, she came up with the winning analogy.

At the final meeting with the agency, when she showed a list of her clients and they said, *But you do not have any previous advertising agency experience,* our rep was ready. *Yes,* she said. *You're right, but let me ask you a question. You just won the Beauty, Inc., account. How much experience did you have to have in the beauty industry to have the right to do their advertising? Let me suggest, the answer is none. You could learn the dynamics of the cosmetics industry, just as you've learned the dynamics of your other accounts in their industries. Beauty, Inc., just had to be sure you were the best advertising agency around. Isn't that true?* They nodded in agreement. *Likewise,* said our rep. *I*

do not have to have previous advertising agency clients to earn your busi-
ness. You just have to be sure I know everything about presentation skills.
And, as you've seen, she concluded, staring them solidly in the eye,
I do.

There was a moment of silence, as the executive vice president
realized that to deny the truth of the analogy would be to utterly
invalidate all the new business the agency had ever pursued. With
the flash of this insight, all the executive vice president could utter
was the single word, *Oh.* The rep won their business and still has
it many years later.

(Someone always asks, *But what if the agency had said they had a
previous big cosmetics account, like Estee Lauder, before Beauty, Inc.?
What would have changed?* Nothing. The rep would have said, "Does
that mean that you didn't have the right to do Estee Lauder's advertising?" The analogy holds.)

The learning point here is that it *pays to plan the placement* of
your various examples, stories, analogies, abstract numbers made
concrete, and quotations or testimonials with your basic Information.

Next, review the cards again and look for the opportunities to
Involve your buyer in your presentation. (Where can you mentally
or actually make the presentation interactive?)

With the addition of these Word Picture and Involvement elements, you may find yourself fine-tuning your Transitions as well.

Finally, review the entire presentation again and decide how
and where you could present this material creatively. (In the Introduction? In the Middle? In the Summary? Stories, props, games,
provocative questions, cartoons, quotations, a theme, unusual
media effects, other?)

Let's take one card from the Middle of the Travel Consultant's
presentation and follow it as it moves from basic information that
tells to information that sells.

1. List Basic Information (📁), visuals, (❯) Transitions.

(Header)	Conference Facilities	
(Info)	• Data on meeting rooms	(pictures)
	• Data on A/V capabilities	
(Transition)	("In addition, . . .")	

2. Decide Key Buyer Points (❗). Decide where to place them. Decide if they will be written, spoken, or both.

(New KBP header)	Great Place for Sales Meetings!
(Info)	◆ Data on meeting rooms (pictures)
	◆ Data on A/V capabilities
(KBP spoken)	*"You will have a hassle-free meeting."*
(Transition)	("In addition, . . .")

3. *Jazz!* it up. Add Word Pictures and Involvement. Fine-tune transitions. Make sure these additions satisfy the *feeling* you want your buyer to have. For example, if you are looking to have your buyer feel "safe" about using your product or service, then pepper your presentation with lots of success stories and testimonials from fairly conservative companies. If you want your buyer to feel "excited" about the possibilities of working with you, bring in stories of your most bizarre successes.

(KBP header)	Great Place for Sales Meetings!
(Info)	◆ Data on meeting rooms (pictures)
(Involve)	(Ask him his A/V needs)
(Info)	◆ Data on A/V capabilities
(Word pix)	(Give examples of different configurations)
(KBP spoken)	"You will have a hassle-free meeting."
(Involve)	(Ask: What does he think?)
(Transition)	"Not only will you have peace of mind, you'll also find . . ."

Now, step back from the entire presentation and look for appropriate ways to be creative in the introduction, middle, or summary. In Meg's case, she wants to do something creative to communicate how much people will love RMR. She decides to do the following: She will get the names of the sixty people who are expected to attend the sales meeting (or the names of the top ten key managers) before she meets with Alex. She will get the same number of picture postcards from the resort and address them to Alex, the meeting planner, with messages that say things like "Great meeting, Alex. Thanks!" "What a gorgeous place you picked. Way to go, buddy!" or "Let's do it again next year!"

She will take these cards to her meeting with Alex and open her presentation by saying, *Alex, how would you like the postman to bring you these after your sales meeting this year?* and then rain the postcards down on Alex's desk. Alternatively, she could close her presentation the same way by saying, *And as a result of coming to RMR this year, Alex, you will have a very successful event. People will love it.* And then rain down the postcards on his desk. Either way, this creative touch will make her point in a memorable way. It's also fun, and the little extra creative thinking that went into her presentation, tailored to Alex, shows him how committed she is to making his meeting a success.

Stage Four: Check Your Presentation's Selling Power

At this stage you switch from being the creator of your presentation to being your own critical coach. This time, when you review the cards and what you intend to say on each, score them with the Jazz! icons (see Figure 9-4) to see if you have really created a presentation that has the music, the elements and flow, most likely to win the business.

Remember, you can write the icons on each page or you can

Figure 9-4. Keeping score with the Jazz! icons.

use different colored Avery dots to ensure that all the elements you want in the presentation are, in fact, there.

Do not confuse the *number* of pages in your presentation with the *elements* of a winning presentation. For example, you may decide to *say* all five elements of an introduction on your single title page. When you score your introduction, all five icons would be on that one page. Alternatively, you may have a separate page for your Buyer's Objectives, Situation, and your Idea. Just make sure that, in either option, what you *say* embodies all the elements of a winning presentation.

To score the middle of your presentation, you can write in the small icons for each element in the half-inch space that you left open on each card. Alternatively, you can use the Avery dots approach to determine the presence or absence of word pictures, involvement techniques, and transitions.

Score your summary with the icons the same way you did your introduction. Then, step back and look at the pattern your entire presentation creates.

Analysis

Is your introduction pattern structured to get you on the beat with your buyer? Will the middle patterns "cook" with buyers? Is your summary pattern structured to move your buyer easily to a close? If the answer is no, then add, eliminate, or change those elements that need to be modified.

Final Selling Power Check

Pilots preparing to take off in a 747 jumbo jet don't trust a final safety check to memory. They use a checklist to make sure everything is ready to go with the airplane. Do a final selling power check on your presentation as well with the following list of questions.

INTRODUCTION

1. Does my opening get my buyer's attention by hitting the Buyer's Objective?

2. Do I briefly review the Buyer's Situation?

3. Does the presentation move naturally with a good Setup Question to my Idea or Recommendation?

4. Is my Idea or Recommendation clear? Does it use language that will hook into my buyer's mind?

5. Do I whet my buyer's appetite for hearing the rest of the presentation by restating the value of my Idea or Recommendation to his objective?

6. If appropriate, have I included an agenda?

7. Have I determined the procedure for questions?

MIDDLE

8. Does my Information anticipate the questions, objections, and points of possible confusion my buyer will have?

9. Is my presentation interesting and easy to understand? Have I included enough examples, stories, analogies, concrete numbers, quotations, or testimonials?

10. Have I made my Information relevant with strong Key Buyer Points?

11. Have I decided how and where I will involve my buyer in the presentation?

12. Have I done anything creative in this presentation to make it have even more impact?

13. Have I made it easy to follow with good Transitions?

SUMMARY

14. Have I made it easy for the buyer to say yes?
    Is there a brief recap of his situation?
    Is there a brief recap of my Idea or Recommendation?
    Is there a brief restatement of the fact that my Idea will help my buyer achieve his objectives?

15. Is there a specific Action Step, and is it appropriate for this buyer?

OVERALL

16. Is the tone right?
17. Will my buyer feel the way I want him to feel?
18. Will this presentation achieve my objective?

Remember that every presentation will be different, but this type of advance Jazz! planning ensures that you've considered all the critical elements you need for a winning presentation.

Rehearsal

If I miss one day's practice, I notice it. If I miss two days' practice, the critics notice it. If I miss three days' practice, the audience notices it.

—Arthur Rubinstein

It's important to run through your presentation several times. It's even better to audiotape or videotape yourself giving the presentation. Add, eliminate, or change any elements as needed.

Summary

1. As the saying goes: "People don't plan to fail, but they often fail to plan"—and that lapse often leads to lost business. Don't take that chance. Be a Jazz! planner.

2. When there is no time to plan, recalling the Jazz! icons and framework will enable you to present a seemingly spontaneous, relevant, interesting, and persuasive presentation on the spot.

3. When there is time to plan, it is useful to follow these four stages to organize your presentation:

    A. Think through basic dynamics:
- your interests
- your buyer's world
- content and visuals
- other considerations

    B. Block out your basic introduction, information, summary, and transitions. Put this rough presentation on large index cards and lay them out so that you can see the whole presentation at once. Walk through the presentation to check its basic flow and order.

C. Jazz! up the presentation. Add Key Buyer Points, Word Pictures, Involvement techniques, and creativity to make your presentation relevant, interesting, and compelling.

D. Check the presentation's selling power. Write in the icons alongside the different elements of your presentation (or use Avery dots). Look at the patterns these icons form in your introduction, in the middle, and in your summary. Make any changes to produce an overall pattern of presentation elements that is robust, dynamic, and persuasive.

4. Rehearse. Go over the presentation several times. Remember: "How do you get to Carnegie Hall?" *"Practice, practice, practice!"*

10

Refine the "Riff"

Tell the Right Story

"I just want to eat! I don't want to see a storyboard of our dinner."

When you use the questions in Chapter 9 to plan and block out your presentation, you will create a very strong presentation. However, it will be even stronger when your Idea or Recommendation is as perfect a fit as possible to your buyer's needs or situation. It's like selecting the most appropriate music to play at a special occasion. No matter how well you can play "Happy Birthday" on the piano, it is still the wrong piece of music to play at midnight for a New Year's Eve party.

Develop the Story

In jazz, a repeating theme or musical phrase is called a "riff." In your presentation, your Idea is the riff, or story behind your presentation. It's a repeating premise that drives the whole presentation. It is stated in your introduction (🔆); it is explained and supported in the middle; and, it is repeated again in the Summary (🔆).

Establishing a Strong Story

Jim Fishman, publisher of *Audubon Magazine,* once observed about his industry that every magazine has a good sales story to tell. A poor story is not the problem. The problem is telling the *right* story to the *right* advertiser at the *right* time. That's the challenge. The same is true for your product or service. No doubt you have a good product or service, but the story about it needs to be the *right* story told the *right* way to the *right* buyer at the *right* time.

The right sales story is not the canned pitch of a novice, which often sounds like this: *We are wonderful. Use our product.* (What did the buyer expect you to say? *Don't use our product. It really isn't very good?*) Nor is a winning story the endless laundry list of features and benefits given as the "story" by most average salespeople. *Use our product, because it has these ten features . . .* Their list only becomes confused in their buyer's mind with the equally impressive laundry lists of competitors.

The right sales story is a carefully crafted, memorable business proposition or rationale stated in your Idea/Recommendation that fits a buyer's specific business situation. It captures the essence of your presentation. Its strength is a function of your understanding of your buyer's situation and the logic, language, and imagery that you use to express your story. A good story lets your buyer know that you listened to him and that you now have a specific, well-thought-out proposition to make.

In Chapter 4, we talked about the power of language to hook your Idea into your buyer's mind, to make it memorable and easy to grasp. We emphasized the value of using catchy phrases and imagery in expressing your Idea or Recommendation ("Service on time, every time," "hot line" to your market). This chapter asks you not only to use imagery, but to make sure that the imagery is part of the most appealing story for each particular buyer.

Regardless of the industry in which you work, your prospects will tend to be in one of three business situations—negative, positive, or neutral:

1. They are facing existing problems.
2. Business has never been better.
3. Business isn't great, but it's okay.

Each of these situations requires a different "story" in your Idea or Recommendation. Buyers with problems want solutions. Buyers who are riding high look for added value. Buyers in the middle need to have their complacency upset, so that they either feel they do have a problem or that they are missing something of real value to them.

There is a fourth category, but it's not usually a good one to pursue. It's the buyer who is not just happy with her current situation; she is ecstatic about it and there's just about nothing she wants. In many businesses, you would call these your "D" accounts, the long shots. With these prospects, you have to wait until they either change jobs or business turns bad. You may want to go after them, but it's going to be a very long-term sell. The investment in time and energy may not be worth it.

We'll look at each of the three more viable sales situations and how they would affect the development and wording of the story in your Idea/Recommendation.

Situation #1

Your buyer is in a problem situation. For example, your buyer's product is a good one, but any or all of the following are also happening: productivity is off; costs are getting out of line; deadlines are being missed; there's adverse publicity; technology has become obsolete; sales are off; market share is down; foreign competition is hurting business; new regulations threaten litigation; performance is poor; resources have been reduced; budgets have been cut; error rates have exploded; etc.

(Which of your current buyers is in this situation?)

You would ask yourself, based on this buyer's situation, what is the best sales story (the best phrased, most logical story to present as my Idea/Recommendation) to show how my product/service can help solve all or part of this client's *problem?*

Return to the Meg and Alex scenario. Become Alex, the meeting planner, and suppose that you are a buyer in a problem situation.

It seems that the sales meeting last year was in a beautiful resort in Florida, but it rained almost all the time, greatly disappointing all the golfers and tennis players in the group; the lodging had wonderful amenities, but the food wasn't very good; the meeting rooms were spacious with great audiovisual support, but there were no windows and people felt claustrophobic. Overall, the meeting was *not* a success and you (the buyer) must find a better place this year. You are fearful of a repeat failure and are looking at a number of possibilities.

Meg's Thinking

Knowing you're in a problem situation, Meg thinks about her presentation this way:

Hmmm, the key here seems to be that I have to make him feel that coming to RMR will be an absolute, unqualified, no-risk success both professionally and personally. Okay, I'll make that the basis for my Idea/ Recommendation (the sales story), and then I'll present specific proof to support what I say and lace the whole presentation with lots of personalized success stories, so that overall, the picture I paint will make Alex feel safe as well as excited about bringing his people here this year. I will repeat this theme of success and safety throughout the presentation. My story will be that choosing RMR is a sure thing.

In the actual presentation, Meg states her Idea this way:

 RMR is the perfect place for you, a surefire choice in every way:

- Guaranteed weather
- Superb amenities and award-winning cuisine
- State-of-the-art meeting facilities that allow views of the Rockies on three sides

 As a result, people will love this meeting. Take a look at what you'll be getting . . .

Then, the middle of the presentation will go into detail and support this particular sales story. Meg's Information and Key Buyer Points will tie back to *assurances* of a good time for everyone and excellent customer service.

She'll show lots of pictures with guests enjoying themselves to reinforce that good feeling. Perhaps each visual will have a testimonial quote on the top from a well-known company to subliminally make Alex feel more comfortable with RMR.

The summary will repeat the sales story stated in the introduction, locking in the principal message of security, support, and guaranteed success that will be appropriate for Alex (the buyer) in this particular situation.

The whole tone of the presentation will be exciting, but very reassuring, and the "surefire" image adds visual impact to Meg's Idea. Now, look how this would change when the buyer's situation is different.

Situation #2

Your buyer is in a positive situation. Sales are up; a new product introduction is a wild success; the buyer has won awards and is opening new markets; performance is up; a litigation case was just won; the company's stock is up, etc.

(Which of your current buyers is in this situation?)

Based on the above information, you would ask yourself, What is the best sales story that would show how my product/service would add value to this client's positive situation?

Return to Meg and Alex. This time Alex is in a positive situation. Business was tough this year, but the company made its numbers and everyone is looking forward to getting away to a beautiful resort and celebrating. Last year's meeting in Florida was a big success. Work sessions are planned for the mornings only. Afternoons and evenings are to be for some well-earned relaxation, sports, and fun. You (the buyer) are looking for a really exceptional time to reward these top, high-charging sales performers.

Meg's Thinking

Knowing you're in a positive situation, Meg thinks about her presentation like this:

These folks are clearly out to have a rip-roaring time after coming off a tough, successful year. I have to make the resort something really special for Alex. I need to paint a highly charged, winners' picture of RMR to show how coming here would really be a true reward for their people and add value to their positive situation. Alex sees these people as tops in their fields, so my story will be to play on a tops *theme.*

Meg states her Idea this way:

 Take your top performers to the "top of the world!" Come to Rocky Mountain Resort:

- *"Tops" in views*
- *"Tops" in activities*
- *"Tops" in luxury*
- *"Tops" in fun!*

As a result, you'll have a meeting that will make your folks feel like they just won the Super Bowl! Take a look at these views from the top of the world. . . .

The rest of the presentation will expand on this story and play off "top," "top of the world," and "top performers." Meg will provide information similar to the first example, but it will be presented differently. Information, Key Buyer Points, and Word Pictures paint RMR as the resort of winners, perhaps where some Olympic athletes stayed. The full range of sports will be described as both relaxing *and* challenging. The best golf courses mentioned will include names of *famous* golf pros. Award-winning cuisine will be included. There will be heavy name-dropping of powerhouse companies that have come to RMR, and stress on special events, like a pro-am golf tournament, for this very important group. Visuals will feature dynamic action pictures.

The summary will repeat the tops story stated in the introduction, and developed and reinforced in the middle of the presentation. Meg will lock in the principal message and feeling of RMR as a unique choice in resorts for winners, for people at the top. Meg will even leave the buyer with a gold toy top as a lasting visual metaphor for RMR.

The whole tone of the presentation will be exciting, but instead of appealing to Alex's needs for safety and guarantees as in the first situation, it will play into Alex's desire to *reward* his winners with a resort *commensurate to their achievements.*

Situation #3

Your buyer's situation is neutral. Business isn't great, but it's okay; the system the buyer is using isn't the latest, but it's adequate; portfolio performance isn't in the top decile, but it's not in the bottom quartile either; the benefits plan is not as inclusive as it might be, but it's acceptable as is; the error rate on the manufacturing line is not the lowest, but it is certainly within acceptable standards; the buyer likes you personally, but he's happy with your competition;

the buyer is very happy using your services at current levels, but doesn't see the need to increase purchases; etc.

(Which of your buyers is in this situation?)

Based on the above information, you would ask yourself, What is the best sales story to justify why the buyer should reconsider my product or service, or reconsider increasing his business with me?

Back to Meg and you, Alex. Only this time, you're in a neutral situation. The company had its meeting in Florida last year. While there were some minor complaints, people were very happy for the most part. They had enough to do, the food was terrific, and the meeting facilities were adequate. Since most people are golfers, it looks like the company will head back to Florida, if not to the same resort, then to any of several similar to it. You see no reason to radically change meeting venues.

Meg's Thinking

Knowing that you were satisfied with what you did last year and are in a neutral situation, Meg's thinking goes like this:

This will not be easy. They are relatively happy, and no one changes what they are doing when they are reasonably content. I have to jar Alex out of complacency either by holding out a greater opportunity or by making him worry that he is missing something. I think I'll try the greater opportunity route and suggest that since their people worked harder last year and produced more for the company, they've earned the right to more of a reward—in Colorado. My story will be the theme of giving the reps more in return for the more business they did this year.

Meg states her Idea this way:

 Your salespeople gave you more in revenues last year. Give them more in their sales meeting this year:

- *More activities*
- *More unusual scenery*
- *More terrific memories*

☺ *As a result, you will have a very successful sales meeting. Just*
>   *look at how much more they can do in Colorado. . . .*

The rest of Meg's presentation will basically show how much more there is to do; how much more people will have to talk about; how much more unique this experience will be for them.

The summary will repeat her Idea stated in the introduction and lock in the principal message of giving the sales team even more of a good time in Colorado than in any other place.

The whole tone of the presentation will be exciting and very seductive, complete with pictures and verbal descriptions to get the meeting planner excited about the possibilities of Colorado and make him forget, or minimize, the attractions of the Florida resort. Meg will even arrange to have satisfied clients, who have also been to Florida resorts, call the buyer to rave about RMR.

In the Spotlight: Your Turn

Consider your presentation. Is your buyer in a problem, positive, or neutral business situation? How strong a story do you have in your Idea or Recommendation in response to that situation? If your buyer is in a positive business situation, does the story in your Idea add value to the buyer? If your buyer is in a problem situation, does the story in your Idea solve that problem? If your buyer is in a neutral situation, does the story in your Idea either tempt him with something better or make him think he is missing something by not using you? In all cases, is the language strong and appealing? Does it use imagery or catchy phrases?

Do you, in fact, have the right story for the right buyer at the right time expressed in the right way? If not, how would you re-work it?

Practice

Select two other buyers who are familiar to you, each of whom is in a different buying situation from the one you just reviewed.

Answer these questions for each buyer to help you decide the best story to put into your Idea or Recommendation for each one.

1. What is his or her business objective? To: _____

2. What is happening in his or her business that is positive?
    *_____
    *_____
    *_____

3. What is happening in his or her business that is negative?
    *_____
    *_____
    *_____

4. Based on the previous information, which buying situation is this buyer in?
    *Positive? Will respond best to an Idea that promises added value to his or her situation.
    *Problem? Will respond best to an Idea that promises a solution for him or her.
    *Neutral? Need to upset his or her complacency. Best way to do that is to show how he or she can get more of something, or that by doing nothing he or she will lose something. I will show what he or she can
    ☐ gain
    ☐ lose
    ☐ (or both?)

5. What is the best proposition, rationale, or "story" to use to express that Idea or Recommendation?

    _____
    _____
    _____
    _____

6. What "hooking" language can I use to give my story impact and make it easy to remember, such as a metaphor or analogy like the "Tiffany" of the business, or a catchy phrase like "on time, on target, on budget"?

Summary

1. You generally find buyers in one of three situations: negative, positive, or neutral.

2. It is worth spending some time to think how you will phrase your Idea or Recommendation to fit those situations, and then to carry the story in your Idea through to the end of your presentation.

3. The difference between telling the right story at the right time to the right buyer and not doing that is the same as the difference between singing a song well or singing it slightly off-key. The listener will recognize the song in both cases, but is more likely to prefer the first one.

11

Play It "in Style"

Customize Your Presentation

"Would you like the technical or the nontechnical presentation?"

"The greatest problem in communication is the illusion that it has been accomplished."
—George Bernard Shaw

Did you ever present to someone who continually raced ahead of you to the last pages before you were ready to show them? Or have you ever been frustrated by a buyer who insisted that you go over every number in every column on a page? You may have found these experiences frustrating, but both of these buyers were giving you clues as to how to present to them to win the business.

These buyers were exhibiting differences in communication styles. People often show you very definite preferences for how they like to receive their information and for how they make decisions. Star salespeople look and listen for these preferences when they are talking to their buyers and build these observations into their presentations.

A communication style is a preferred way of receiving and processing information. Styles have different tempos and fairly different predictable ways of making decisions. There are four styles. All of us have a combination of those four styles, but we usually tend to prefer one or two of the four. No one style is better or worse than another. A style is simply a *preference*; it is not a measure of someone's value or intelligence. You always think your style is best, but it isn't. It's like having blue eyes or brown eyes. A style is neither good nor bad; it's just what it *is*.

The Styles Defined

As you review the following thumbnail sketches of each style, you'll recognize these four styles immediately in yourself and in people you know. As you review these descriptions, identify someone you know—account, spouse, boss, friend, or child—who has a lot of each particular style. It will help you remember the styles more easily.

For purposes of easy reference, we'll call the four styles the computer, the friend, the bullet, and the pinball machine.

The Computer

Has a preference for facts: Likes to hear how what you are saying is logical; makes sense; has all loose ends tied up; is justified by the data; gets results in an orderly, rational, logical way

Clues to this Style: Slower speaking tempo; little small talk; may appear cold or aloof; has concerns about process, specifics, and details

Typical questions:

Why is the fourth number in the third column only 20 and not 20.5?

Can you get me more information on that?

How do you monitor effectiveness?

Hot button words/phrases: Control, monitor, process, check, solid, research-based, evidence shows, exact, accurate, thorough, scientific, systematic, factored in, components, rationale

Needs/appreciates: Businesslike tone, data, charts, graphs, an objective approach, patience, time to digest, logical arguments, details

Effective Action Steps: Remember, these are orderly thinkers.

Mr. Buyer,

- *What is our next step?*
- *Let me leave this with you to review. Can we set up a meeting on Tuesday to discuss the next step?*
- *Did I omit any information that you need to help you make your decision?* (No.) *Then, what do you see as our next step?* or (Yes. I need to know . . .) *Fine. I will get that to you today. Can we meet on Tuesday to determine the next step?*

Who do you know who has strong computer characteristics?

The Friend

Has a preference for relationships: Likes to hear how what you are saying will improve relationships, build a team, develop good feelings, is a sure thing, risk-free, guaranteed, easy to do, helpful to others

Hot button words/phrases: Feel, feelings, people, loyalty, trust, positive image, team, fun, lively, no worry, reliability, together as a team, group or family, safe, proven, consensus

Clues to this Style: Warmth, openness, interest in you, lots of small talk, always available, concerns for people in company

Typical questions:

Who else have you done this with?

Who will be handling my business?

What happens if there's a problem?

What did the other committee members say?

Needs/appreciates: People-oriented visuals, humor, warmth, fun, vitality, laughter, concern, compassion, sincerity, success stories of others who have used your products or services, reassurance

Effective Action Steps: Remember, these are consensus-oriented people.

Mr. Buyer,

+ *The next step is to set up a meeting with the committee. Would you like to arrange that?*
+ *I'm delighted that you like this . . . so much. Should we begin the analysis on Monday or is there someone else you want me to see?*
+ *The next step is to do . . . Who else should I see to move this forward for you?*

Who do you know who has strong friend characteristics?

The Bullet

Has a preference for action: Likes to hear how what you are saying gets the job done, works in the shortest amount of time possible, gets results, solves the problem. This is your Type A personality.

Hot button words/phrases to use: Bottom line, net-net, what this means is, done, right away, no hassle, get to it, no problem, we can do it, done deal, your return on investment will be . . .

Clues to this style: You feel pressured. They are very goal-oriented and very competitive. Little to no interest in you personally. They cut you off in mid-sentence.

Typical questions:

How fast can you get this up and running?
When can I have it?
What's your point?

Needs/appreciates: Short meetings, getting to the point quickly, focus on results, not process, humor/wit, directness, simple visuals

Effective Action Steps: Remember, they are action-oriented.

Mr. Buyer,

+ *When do you want to start?*
+ *I recommend we start Tuesday. Can you do it then?*
+ *What do you want to do next?*

Who do you know with strong bullet characteristics?

The Pinball Machine

Has a preference for ideas and the big picture: Likes to hear how what you are saying fits into the big picture; is innovative, creative, exciting, different;

fits in with the long term; how it's connected to other things; how it throws new light on things; how it will change, revolutionize, transform their product, market, business, situation

Hot button words/phrases: Synergies, big picture, integrate, fascinating, unique, once in a lifetime, provocative, possibilities, growth, trends, long-term, new, first, unusual

Needs/appreciates: Big ideas, creativity in a presentation, creative visuals, information presented in unusual ways, prestigious testimonials, an upbeat feel to the presentation

Clues to this Style: Their minds work like pinball machines, jumping from topic to topic. You feel confused. They take little personal interest in you. They care about the future. They are creative. They may seem a little odd.

Typical questions:
> *What if we did this another way?*
> *How does this relate to the other divisions?*
> *What are the trends here?*

Effective Action Steps: Remember, they love the big picture and are weak on details.
> Mr. Buyer,
> • *Let's take out our calendars and set a date now for next week.*
> • *Who do you want me to see to work out the details?*

Who do you know with strong pinball machine characteristics?

Did you recognize yourself? Did you recognize people you know? Then you also realize that we are all a mix of styles. However, when one or more style preferences in a buyer becomes apparent to you, it's wise to respond to that preference in your presentation.

Styles in Action

Using the RMR case, let's say that Meg, the travel consultant, wants to present the fact that RMR has ten different meeting rooms that can be configured any way the buyer needs them to be.

If the buyer's style was clearly oriented toward the **computer** (information) style, she might say,

You get ten different meeting rooms at RMR. The walls are retractable, which allows us to systematically *divide the rooms to* your specifications. *You can have four small breakouts for your Monday meetings*

with seatings of up to twenty-five in each room, two larger settings for your Tuesday sessions with seatings of up to fifty in each room, and one large ballroom size for your awards evening dinner with seating up to 125.

If the buyer was clearly oriented toward the **friend** (relationships) style, Meg might say,

You get ten different meeting rooms at RMR with retractable walls, which allow you to create any room size and feeling *that you want for your group. For example, on Monday, you can have four breakout rooms,* conducive to team-building and sharing of feelings, thoughts, and ideas, *for your smaller groups. On Tuesday, two larger settings can be created for up to fifty people each.* We can put circular tables in there for groups of six so people will be able to talk to each other more easily. Then, for your awards dinner, we'll do a beautiful ballroom arrangement for you, complete with personal name cards and tables for eight to ten, whichever way you think people would like it best.

If the buyer was clearly oriented toward the **bullet** (action) style, she might say,

The meeting arrangements are a snap. *Retractable walls allow us to give you* whatever *configuration you want. Tell us when, how many, and we do it!*

If the buyer was clearly oriented to the **pinball** machine (big picture and possibilities) style, Meg might say,

There are many room configuration possibilities. *Retractability gives you* amazing flexibility. *Four meetings of up to twenty-five, with* any kind *of seating you want. Two meetings with up to fifty each, again with any seating. We can keep the same color* themes *throughout* or vary them *with the meetings. Then, for the awards night* extravaganza, *the decor can become* very elegant at one extreme or very Wild West fun at the other extreme, or maybe a combination of both! *Whatever you* envision *for your group, we can create for you.*

And if the buyer was clearly a combination of styles, for example, the **pinball machine** and the **bullet,** Meg would combine the two and change the last sentence in the previous example to:

Bottom line, you see *it, we* do *it!*

Caution: Don't go overboard with styles. Most people need satisfaction in all four styles. They need the facts. They want to have

a positive feeling toward the salesperson. They like to see the possibilities of what they are buying. And they want to know what
results they'll get. It's only when you really notice a *strong* preference for one or more of the styles that you'll want to put some extra
effort into satisfying that buyer's need for how he or she prefers to
hear what you are saying.

In the Spotlight: Your Turn

1. Select four real buyers, each with an observable different
style preference.

2. Select *one* piece of information that you would normally
present about your product or service. It can be a description of
your product or service, how it works, the results of some research,
a cost-benefit analysis, or how you compare to competitors.

3. Using the previous guidelines, present that piece of information to fit the strongest style of each of those buyers. Take into
account the language and tempo you use; the Key Buyer Points
you make; the degree of detail you go into; the Word Pictures you
give; any appropriate creative extras you want to add; and the action step you request.

4. Tape yourself. Then, listen to the tape as if you were each of
the buyers. Do you see how your responsiveness to *their* different
thinking styles would increase your selling power with each of
them?

Knowing what you now know about different communicating
style preferences, can you think of a past lost sales call where a
greater sensitivity to your buyer's style might have won the business?

Your Presentation Style: Power or Pitfall?

"The fault, dear Brutus, lies not in the stars, but in ourselves."
—from *Julius Caesar*

We talked about your buyers' styles, but what about *your* style
preferences and how they affect the way you present? Remember,

we are all a mix of styles. There is no better style. However, any style strength carried to an extreme can become a weakness. Review the chart in Figure 11-1 and determine strengths and potential weaknesses of your presentation style.

Polish Up Your "Style"

As you review Figure 11-1, you no doubt see yourself in all four categories. That is not surprising. You also see potential presentation pitfalls. Review the suggestions in Figure 11-2 for transforming the weaknesses you uncovered into selling power strengths.

As you would imagine, the concept of style preferences applies in all types of relationships: marriages, families, management, friendships, or task forces. While it is fun to explore the implications of style in all these areas, for our purposes think about styles in connection with your presentations. Be appreciative of your style strengths as well as sensitive to their dangers.

(text continues on page 188)

Figure 11-1. Your style: power or pitfall.

Strong Data Preference	
+	−
Organized, logical, thorough	May seem aloof
Well prepared	Doesn't relate information to
Steady with difficult buyers	client's world
Gives clinically correct	Goes into too much detail
presentations	Often misses client cues
Plans well	Doesn't use enough Word
Highly credible	Pictures
	Doesn't involve buyer
	Tells, doesn't sell
	Gets lost in visuals

(continues)

Figure 11-1. (Continued)

Strong Relationships Preference	
+	**−**
Makes people comfortable	Becomes defensive easily
Involves buyers	Doesn't close strongly
Works for harmony	Poor sense of time passing
Sets presentations up well	Personalizes objections
Can make presentations fun	May tell too many personal stories

Strong Action Preference	
+	**−**
High energy	May seem aggressive, rude
Strong on Key Buyer Points	Cuts people off
Goes for closure/commitment	Creates feelings of pressure
Can adapt to changes quickly	Becomes combative in Q & A
	Doesn't plan

Strong Ideas Preference	
+	**−**
Has creative, curious mind	Talks at, not with, people
Strong with analogies	Often rambles and loses buyer
Generates excitement	Often insensitive to others
Sees big picture	May seem "odd"
Finds it easy to be creative	May confuse buyers

Figure 11-2. From pitfall to power.

If You Tend to Be the Computer
After you explain something, practice using a mix of phrases like, *Which means you get . . .,* or *So what this means to you is . . .,* or *Bottom line, you'll get . . .* This will ensure that your buyer sees the relevance of what you're saying.
When you block out your presentations, aim for at least one example on every page of Information in the presentation. This will keep your material interesting for your buyer.
When you are practicing, aim for the key ideas on a page, as opposed to a remedial reading of every word and number. This will keep your buyer's attention.

If You Tend to Be the Friend

Practice a strong, specific Action Step, so that when it comes time to close, you are ready. Helpful phrases are: *Mr. Buyer, the next step would be to . . . Would you like to do that?* or *Mr. Buyer, what would you like me to do next?* or *"Mr. Buyer, what's our next step?"* These phrases are all buyer-centered and nonpressuring to make closing easier for you.

Tell stories about other satisfied clients rather than about yourself. Your buyers will more readily believe and identify with those accounts than with your experience.

Do a time check with people before you present, so that you know just how much time you have and can act accordingly. No one ever becomes annoyed if you finish a presentation five minutes early, but everyone gets irritated if you run even a minute over (particularly those bullet and computer types!).

If You Tend to Be the Bullet

Give more time to planning your presentations. They will be more successful for you.

Recognize that not everyone paces as quickly as you do, so slow down when you are explaining things. Pause after key points, so that they sink in with your buyer, before you race off to the next point.

Allow people to finish their questions. Even though you may know what is coming, people are offended when you insist on repeatedly cutting them off. Listen patiently. People will feel less pressured and more positive about working with you.

If You Tend to Be the Pinball Machine

Give yourself more planning time. Buyers feel better when they can hear a clear beginning, middle, and end of a presentation.

Since this style tends to jump in random fashion from idea to idea, particularly during questions and answers, remember this phrase, *So, therefore . . .* It will generally snap you back to a point. This makes it easier for your buyer to follow your thoughts.

Identify a specific action step that you want from the presentation, practice it, and make sure to include it in your meeting, perhaps with its own visual aid so it doesn't get forgotten.

Summary

1. People have different communicating style preferences: Ideas, Relationships, Data, and Action.
2. People with similar styles tend to "get" what the other person is saying easily and quickly. People with different styles frequently miscommunicate.
3. Star presenters recognize and respond to the communication style preferences of their buyers.
4. Star presenters also recognize the power and pitfalls of their own style, accept the former, and work on managing the latter.

You've composed your sales music. Your presentation is relevant, interesting, memorable, persuasive, and tailored to your buyer. You've practiced. If you are presenting to one or two people, you are probably fairly calm. However, if you are *playing* before an audience of several buyers, you are likely to have performance jitters. Learn how to *play it cool* in a group situation in Chapter 12.

12

Play It "Cool"

How to Survive Group Presentations

REHEARSAL

What's your favorite active sport? Tennis? Skiing? Aerobics? Jogging? How about presenting?

The dynamics in sports and presenting are very similar. They're both physical (you're doing something). They're both psychological (your mindset impacts your performance). They're both emotionally challenging (you experience anxiety before you *play*). Finally, you perform better in both when you've prepared and practiced prior to playing.

Performance jitters usually hit at four times: the night before, the morning of, the moments just prior to (stage fright), and the first few moments of the actual presentation. This is perfectly normal. However, what you want is a way to manage these anxieties so that they energize, rather than paralyze, you in the presentation.

Jitters the Night Before

In his book, *I Can't Accept Not Trying*, Michael Jordan, perhaps basketball's greatest player ever, says, "If I'm going to jump into a pool of water, even though I can't swim, I'm thinking about being able to swim, at least enough to survive. If I'm jumping into any situation, I'm thinking I'm going to be successful. I'm not thinking about what happens if I fail."*

Like all performers, whether you are on the field, on the stage, or in the boardroom, you must put yourself in a positive mindset. The power of a negative thought to undermine your confidence is deadly. Before you retire for the evening, reread those thank-you letters from clients. Remind yourself that you can do this presentation, that you've prepared, that you're a professional, that you represent a fine product or service, that your client will benefit from what you're selling, and that you've made other clients happy with your product or service. Don't be modest. Really lay it on.

Another positive sports/performance technique is visioning, seeing the positive result of your actions and imagining the plea-

---

*Michael Jordan, *I Can't Accept Not Trying* (New York: HarperCollins). Reprinted by permission of HarperCollins Publishers, Inc.

sure that comes with that result. See yourself doing the presentation. See your client responding positively to it. See your client saying *yes*. Imagine yourself feeling good about the meeting. In short, psych yourself up to win.

A positive mindset is good. A perfectionist mindset is disastrous. If you think your only options are failure or perfection, you will work yourself up into an unnecessary frenzy. You don't need to give a perfect presentation. You need to give a *winning* presentation. A word stumbled over, an example forgotten, or a single "um" will ruin a perfect presentation score, but those minor errors will be overwhelmingly outweighed by a fundamentally sound presentation, an enthusiasm for your product and service, and an obvious commitment on your part to help the buyer get what he or she needs to win.

What's Your Worst Nightmare?

Is it that you'll forget something? If it's really important, clients will ask a question. Is it that your mind will go blank? If that happens, stop. Pause to regroup your thoughts. If nothing comes back to you, very matter-of-factly say you've lost your thought and move on. (The thought generally returns very shortly when you do that; then weave the thought back into the presentation.) Is it that you won't know the answer to something? Say you'll get that information and move on. Is it that you'll fumble your words or mix up your thoughts? Say, *Excuse me. Let me back up.* And begin again. Is it that you won't get the business? You can always try again or go to another customer. Even the best players don't win every game.

Keep your perspective. *No one ever died from giving a sales presentation!*

Jitters in the Morning

Continue the positive self-talk from the night before. Since the opening of a presentation is when people are most nervous, repeat your opening lines a few times as you are showering or getting dressed. Become comfortable with them. Don't worry that they won't come out exactly as practiced. If you review them a few times, the gist of your opening will be communicated. Finally, remember that clients don't know what you prepared to say!

Jitters in the Lobby

I freely admit I have never been part of a football huddle, but it's rumored that when those players have their arms around each other before a game, they aren't saying, *Hey, we're going to lose! Right?* No! They are psyching themselves up to win! Do the same for yourself. Continue to tell yourself you will do well.

One salesperson recognized that her presales presentation anxiety was rapidly turning into panic as she was standing in the lobby of her client's building. She did her version of the football huddle. She called up a business friend, frantically admitted she was a wreck, and asked the friend to tell her how wonderful she was. The friend obliged by saying, *You're terrific. You're great. Your clients love you. You can do it. You're better than the competition. You'll win.* As she traveled up nineteen floors in the elevator, this salesperson kept repeating to herself, *I'm terrific. I'm wonderful. I can do this. I'm terrific. I'm wonderful. I can do this.* (Fortunately, the elevator was empty.) When she emerged from the elevator, she *believed* and was able to walk into the office feeling strong and confident. She won the business.

Warm-Ups

Just as athletes, singers, and musicians warm up before playing, you need to warm up before a presentation. Try these three simple, fail-safe presentation warm-ups as you are walking down the hall.

1. Breathe deeply through your nose into your belly to the slow count of eight. Pause. Then exhale through your mouth to the slow count of eight, concentrating on relaxing

your neck, back, and shoulders. Repeat two or three times. When we're nervous, the first thing that goes is our breathing, so this easy exercise is a very critical one to do. It will center and calm you.

2. Hum to yourself to warm up your vocal cords.
3. Yawn a very exaggerated yawn to relax all your facial muscles. (This is best done in the privacy of an empty elevator or in the rest room.)

Jitters in the Room

Work the crowd. In addition to arriving early to check out the logistics of the meeting room, use that informal time to establish familiarity with several individuals if there is a pre-meeting coffee. Introduce yourself, say you are looking forward to the meeting and casually ask what that person is expecting from your presentation. If he mentions something you will be discussing, say, *Good. We will be talking about that.* If he mentions something you will not be discussing, say, *We won't be talking exactly about that, but we will be touching on something related to it.* Or *Would you bring that up in Q & A?* If he says that he has no expectations, simply assure him that he will find the meeting of value for his company.

In all cases, tactfully disengage and repeat this exercise with as many people as possible. Then, when you are standing before the group, you will feel that you know these people and they won't seem so intimidating. These apparently innocent pre-meeting amenities also allow you to personalize your remarks. For example, when you get to something one of these people mentioned in your casual conversation with them, it will be easy to say, *How we implement this will be particularly important to those of you in marketing who face ever shrinking closing deadlines for your campaigns.* Your buyers will appreciate that you listened to them and that you are really working in their best interests and not just getting through the presentation.

As you are settling into your seat, or are just a few seconds away from having to stand and begin your presentation, visualize the first opening Jazz! icon ☺ and it will automatically cue you to your opening line.

When All Else Fails

Fake it. Physically act as if you are feeling great. Recall a time when you experienced success or felt terrific and assume the physicality of that time. Stand the way you felt. Assume the facial expression you felt at that moment. Walk the way you felt. Last, smile. It's hard to think negative thoughts when you're smiling. (Try it.) It's hard to be perceived as timid when you speak up with authority. It's hard to be seen as a wimp when you shake someone's hand strongly and look that person straight in the eye. Remember, when you think you can't make it psychologically, fool your mind and fake it physically. You will feel much better.

A related technique that works for other people is to think of something that makes them feel calm, happy, and upbeat: their kids, a recent vacation, pizza (why not?), a time when they experienced a victory, a previous big sale, zipping down a ski slope, or riding in the country.

The First Few Seconds

These are the most nerve-racking. You may feel your hands sweat, your mouth go dry, your mind go blank, or your heart start to pound. That's your adrenalin getting your body ready for the presentation. It's the same adrenalin that gets your heart going before any competitive game. It's good. It's normal. It helps you play at your best. (Ever hear the story of the matador who was killed on the only day he wasn't nervous.) Also, keep in mind that the audience does not see these things happening to you.

Control is all about breathing and eye contact.

Stand in front of your group. Be silent for a couple of seconds (an eternity to you, but nothing to your audience). Breathe. Instead of sweeping the room with your eyes, like a lighthouse, say your first line looking at one person. Randomly glide to another person for your second line. And so forth. Breathe at the end of sentences.

Pause at the end of important points. A variation is to glide to the next person at the end of a phrase, or when you feel your voice fold down on a thought. This one-to-one communication gives you control over your material and a comfortable, conversational tone to what you're saying.

(Pick friendly looking people in the beginning. Remember that many people who listen intently often look angry. Don't let that throw you. They're not angry; they're just intent on listening.) If you need to look away to collect a thought, that is okay. Just return to the person you left and complete the thought, as you would in a conversation with friends.

Some people find it useful to use the pattern of the baseball field as a way to ensure balanced eye contact with a group. You might start with the person sitting at the equivalent of second base, randomly move to the person in the outfield, then to the person at third base, shift to the person in the infield, next to the outfield, back to first, etc. Just keep your contacts random. For example,

(To person A): *This morning, we want to look at a strategy to help you market XYZ's new product.* (natural breath)
(To B): *XYZ is in an interesting position.* (voice folds down)
(To C): *On the one hand, your product has breakthrough technology,* (natural breath)
(To D): *But it is not well understood and appears too risky for what are fairly conservative buyers.* (natural breath)
(To B): *So, how can we increase their comfort level?* (short pause)
(To A): *Our recommendation is . . .*

Practice this at home. Place pillows at different points in your living room and talk to each pillow for about the length of a phrase or a sentence and then glide on to another pillow. Audiotape yourself to prove that this gives you more control and that you sound authoritative and confident.

With strong eye contact and time for breathing, you will also eliminate an annoying distraction, the time-fillers. These are words that add nothing to the presentation but are said to fill the silence until you find your next thought. *Uh, um, okay, right, you know,* and *like* are time-fillers. When you get to the end of a sentence or thought, simply pause, rather than stick in the time-filler. The silence will seem endless to you, when in reality, it is not noticed by your buyer at all. You will sound more authoritative, professional, and convincing.

Be in the Moment

Players come into a game having practiced, with the desire to win and the expectation of winning. However, when they are actually playing, they allow themselves a *forgetting of self* and concentrate only on the point being played at that moment. To worry or to get excited about the outcome, or about how they look, during a point splits the concentration and usually results in losing the point. Forget yourself and concentrate on getting your point across to your buyer.

Make It a Conversation, Not a Monologue

In a social situation, it is highly unlikely that you would do a monologue for twenty or more minutes without getting some response from the other person. The same is true in selling to a group. You need feedback to know if you are on track. They need a chance to participate to ensure that their needs and concerns are being addressed. There are many ways to do this, depending on the situation.

1. In a small group, after you review your understanding of their situation in your introduction, pause and ask if anyone wants to add anything to that or if anything has changed since you last saw them.
2. At the end of the introduction, ask if there's anything they would like to add to the agenda, if there is one, or have you emphasize.
3. At the end of the introduction, encourage them to ask questions as *we* go through this information.

4. Invite them to ask questions after a particularly complex or controversial exhibit in your presentation.
5. As you are presenting your supporting information in the middle of the presentation, appropriately involve them in the various ways discussed in Chapter 3.
6. In very large group presentations, say twenty-five plus people, it wouldn't be feasible to do #1 or #2, but you could do #3 and #5.

Body Parts

In front of small or large groups, most people get nervous and suddenly wonder what to do with their hands, feet, body, and eyes. Grown adults who never have problems with these in one-on-one conversations suddenly become weak like rag dolls or stiff like ironing boards.

Most books and courses exploit this fear and provide separate lists of *do's* and *don'ts* for your hands, eyes, body, and voice. No wonder you get nervous. Now you have that many more things to think about during the presentation!

However, the real key to the body parts issue is to do one thing: Forget them! It's like walking up a flight of stairs. When you ascend a flight of stairs, you're only thinking about the goal (getting to the top), not what your feet are doing. Miracle of miracles, your feet manage to get you there. In a presentation, think about your goal: getting your buyers turned on to the value of your product or service to help them reach their goals, and, equally miraculous, your body parts will all work just fine, thank you.

Allow me to prove this to you. Try this quick exercise.

Stand in front of a mirror and tell the mirror your name, company name, and business address in your normal speaking voice. Notice how you look. Now, do this again with one change. Using the same words, force yourself to get really excited about your name, company name, and business address. Really push the old enthusiasm button. Go over the top. How does that feel? Dumb? Awkward? Unnatural? Of course. You're being totally unnatural and you're simply listing information.

Now stand in front of the mirror again. This time, think of some issue on which you have a strong point of view, for example, the size of government, the environment, education, television violence, gun control, or lost airline luggage. Assume you are talking to a group of friends who have the opposite point of view. Further assume that if you can change their minds, you will win $1,000 cash. Now, looking in the mirror, talk to these people for about two to three minutes on your topic. As you are speaking, notice how you feel and look.

How did that feel compared to how you felt when you were being artificially excited about your name, company name, and business address? Probably much more natural. The point is that when you have something of value to say and you focus on getting your point across to someone rather than on what you look like, you feel perfectly fine. You weren't thinking about what you were doing. You were just doing it.

Body Parts and Just Doing It

What physical changes did you notice from the time when you just said your name, company name, and address to this last time when you were presenting your point of view? What was different about your eyes and facial expression? Were they more animated? What was different about your hands? Did you use them naturally in gestures in front of you to reinforce your points? What was different about your voice? Did it have more inflection and variety to it? Where was your sense of direction? Were you on the heels of your feet or leaning a bit forward on the balls of your feet? Did you feel more energized or alive?

You were just talking and, eureka!, your eyes, hands, voice, facial expression, and body all worked quite naturally. You probably also had more natural conviction, excitement, and energy in your entire delivery. You were doing what you had to do to get your points across.

Your eyes, hands, voice, and body all actively work together quite naturally when you speak with genuine feeling. That energy travels across the table or across the room to your listeners and is felt by them. It's interesting to note that the root of the word *enthuse* means "to catch fire." When you are excited by what your product or service can do for your clients, when you are caught up in helping them see its value, when you delight in making it easy for them to understand its rewards, your delivery skills take a quantum leap forward and your buyers more readily catch the fire of your message. In sports, you don't play a game with just one part of you, for example, your arm in tennis or your hands in basketball. You play the game with your whole physical being. The same is true in presenting.

There are two delivery tips that inexperienced group presenters can use in the body parts department. The first is to allow themselves to "play the game" more fully when they are presenting, to put more energy into what they are doing than when they are simply sitting across a desk talking to one person.

In sports, you play at a higher energy level during a game than you do when you are merely walking to the field or court. You want to communicate at a higher energy level in group situations. That means projecting your voice *further*, making your gestures *larger*, pausing for effect just a tad *longer* than you might in one-on-one conversation. You don't have to become a cheerleader or perform like an evangelical preacher, but you do want to extend your circle of energy beyond the person sitting in front of you to hold the entire room. Again, practice presenting at this higher energy level in front of a mirror. Although you may feel that you are going over the top, you'll see that you are, in fact, more effective as a communicator.

The second has to do with your hands. In front of a group, many people will put their hands in their pockets, behind their backs, cross their arms across their chests, or hold their hands across the lower part of their bodies, a position known as the "fig leaf." None of these positions is effective. At best, they cut you off from your audience; at worst, they can make you look hostile or uncomfortable. People assume these postures to control nervous energy, but that holding in of anxiety will only make you more tense.

Again, think sports, in which your hands are always somewhere in front of you, at about hip level, ready for action. Your arms are open, not crossed. And when you are not using your hands, they find a resting place in front of your body ready for the next demand on them in the game. Try skiing with your poles crossed in front of you, tennis or squash with your hands and racquet behind you, running with your hands in the fig leaf position; you can't do it and play the sport well. Similarly, keep your hands loosely available for the next point you will make in the presentation.

Final, Reassuring Tip

My experience with thousands of salespeople and management executives is that it's exhausting and unnecessary to worry about all the delivery skills that could go wrong. People generally need to improve in only one or two things to be stronger group presenters. That's because all these skills are connected. An improvement in one or two areas will always have unexpected beneficial effects on your overall delivery. Videotape yourself or have someone listen to you present. You will see that this is true.

For example, maybe you talk too quickly. Practice longer eye contact, slowing down, and pausing more. Not only will you be easier to follow, but you'll be pleasantly surprised to find that your breathing and control will naturally improve as well. Perhaps you fidget. Use your hands more for gestures. As you allow yourself to do that, you'll notice that your voice will also naturally gain greater inflection. You'll also be calmer because you will be burning off nervousness in the gestures.

When you strengthen your eye contact, you tend to focus all your energy toward an individual. This generally leads to an unconscious use of the hands, better inflection, and more natural breathing.

When you project your voice further because you are working at a higher energy level, you will tend to automatically use your hands more, move more, become more animated, and feel less nervous—all just because you are projecting more. It is common for those distracting time-fillers to disappear as well.

Additional suggestions for improving in the one or two areas that you determine need improvement are at the end of this chapter.

Is Delivery Really That Important?

Yes and no. In a perfect world buyers would decide solely on the facts. However, in a human world, buyers are also influenced by *how* that information is communicated. If you appear enthusiastic, interested in your buyer, and speak with conviction, you will be forgiven many small textbook distractions, such as holding onto a pen. However, if you appear lethargic, disinterested, or fidgety, your buyers will lose interest and confidence in what you are saying and those little distractions will become magnified to them.

Return to sports. Imagine you have a regular Tuesday night tennis or squash game with a friend. You're on the court. You serve the ball. It is out of range of your friend, but he could get it if he ran for it. Only he doesn't. You serve again. The same thing happens. You're winning, but assuming you know he is not sick, how do you feel toward him? Angry? Annoyed? Disappointed? Eager for the hour to be over? All of the above? The same is true in presenting. You owe *100 percent* of your energy and attention to your buyer during your presentation. Anything less and your buyer has every right to lose interest in both you and your recommendations.

Finally, think of how the delivery styles of these people affected their ability to get support for their ideas: George Bush, Michael Dukakis, Bob Dole, Martin Luther King, Jr., Ronald Reagan, and Margaret Thatcher.

President Lyndon Johnson once said, "What convinces is conviction. Believe in the argument you are advancing. If you don't, you're as good as dead. The other person will sense something isn't there and no chain of reasoning, no matter how logical or elegant or brilliant, will win your case for you." If that fundamental conviction is missing, no amount of phony delivery skills will win for you, either.

Your Three Best Defenses Against Jitters

1. *Play Jazz!* The Jazz! framework promotes strong delivery skills. Almost no one, and certainly no one in sales, is a natural monotone. However, when a person's presentation pattern is of the Chopsticks variety—a weak introduction and summary, and a middle weighted overwhelmingly with only information—it's hard to come across enthusiastically. With that pattern, you're likely to sound as interesting as you did when you were reciting your name, company, and company address.

When a person's pattern is of the Muzak variety—an average introduction and summary, and a middle that has a pattern of information plus a few word pictures and key buyer points—the delivery is better, but rarely is it really electrifying.

When you play Jazz! in your presentation, you create a strong introduction and summary, and a middle with information that is also rich in key buyer points, word pictures, involvement, smooth transitions, and creativity. You now have the best opportunity to be a dynamic presenter.

2. *Practice.* Review your presentation several times. Become familiar and comfortable with it. Practice your answers to anticipated difficult questions. Listen to yourself on audiotape or videotape, or present it to a colleague for feedback. Edit, modify, or change as necessary. If the Michael Jordans of the world have to practice (and we suspect Michael knows how to play his game), then sales professionals would do well to practice before they have to play *their* game as well.

3. *Think Conversation.* When they hear the word *presentation*, many people immediately snap into an imagined, artificial, and rigid physical posture that only makes them more stiff and more nervous. Change your perception of what you are doing. Replace the word *presentation* and think of what you are doing as *conversation*. To be sure, it is a structured and higher energy conversation, but it is, nevertheless, a conversation. In a conversation, we relate to people and try to help them understand something. In a presentation, we tend to recite and lose our individual vitality. Think that

you're *just talking*. That shift in thinking is often the best antidote for anxiety.

One of the most gratifying moments as a seminar leader I ever had was watching a young Chinese woman in Singapore internalize this shift in perception. In front of everyone's eyes, she went from being a withdrawn, insecure looking presenter to an engaging, captivating communicator. The victory for her was all the more sweet, because culturally she had been taught to be far less forthcoming and direct than Americans normally are. When she looked at herself on videotape, she positively beamed with pleasure at what she was able to do by *just talking*.

Summary

1. Everyone has some degree of performance jitters. They're normal. They're healthy. They're ultimately good for you. See the act of presenting as a sport and treat these jitters in a similar fashion.

2. Channel those jitters into dynamic delivery power:
   A. Prepare. Use the principles embodied in the Presentation Jazz! system to structure the flow and logic of your presentation.
   B. Practice the presentation five or six times.
   C. Practice your responses to any expected hard questions.
   D. Use positive self-talk to psyche yourself up.
      * See yourself being successful to create a self-fulfilling prophecy.
      * Review your opening several times to increase your comfort level.
      * Breathe deeply to calm down.
      * Hum to warm the vocal cords.
      * Yawn to release tension.
      * Use conversational, one-to-one eye contact to give you control over your breathing and your material.

- Stay focused in the moment with your buyers to be natural.
- Be enthusiastic and upbeat to help your buyers catch the fire in your message.

Although you may not be able to shoot baskets like Michael Jordan, you can take advantage of the advice he gives in his book:

> I think fear sometimes comes from a lack of focus or con-
> centration, especially in sports. If I had stood at the free-
> throw line and thought about 10 million people watching
> me on the other side of the camera, I couldn't have made
> anything. . . . Any fear is an illusion. You think something
> is standing in your way, but nothing is really there. What
> *is* there is an opportunity to do your best and gain some
> success.*

Exercises

The following exercises and tips will help you "play it cool" before group sales meetings:

To Reduce Tension
1. Lift your shoulders up as high as you can, hold for eight seconds and drop them quickly. Repeat.
2. Tighten your fists for five seconds as hard as you can. Then quickly open. Repeat three times.
3. Exercise that morning.
4. Some people need caffeine to get them going; others find it makes them jumpy. Decide which category you fit into and take, or avoid, accordingly.

To Build Voice Inflection
1. Select a simple sentence, such as *She said he loves to travel.* Then, repeat the sentence four times with the emphasis on a different word each time. *She said he loves to travel. She* said *he loves to travel. She said he* loves *to travel. She said he loves to* travel. The meaning changes with each emphasis. Do this with other sentences and tape yourself. See how much

*Ibid.

more interesting, dramatic, and effective you can be with varying voice inflection.

2. Read aloud five to ten minutes daily. Get used to hearing your own voice. Tape yourself. Practice different levels of enthusiasm; you'll see how much room you have for genuine conviction.

3. Stand in front of a mirror and *sell* yourself on your product, using your hands freely to reinforce your points.

4. Use your hands to count, to show spatial relationships, to show movement or processes, and for emphasis. Exaggerate as if you were playing charades. (*There are* three *reasons why this strategy works:* one . . ., two . . ., three. . . . *The market is* big, *but when you* narrow *it down, you get* . . . We began . . . *ten years ago, then, we moved to* . . . *five years ago until today, we are* here . . . The key point to remember is that *only* XYZ Company can do both operations for you.)

Audiotape yourself. What you'll notice is that when you use your hands, your voice inflection always improves. Also, you'll see how large the playing field is for your hands to make a point, describe a process, count off benefits, or describe how something works.

Make all your gestures in front of you in an area between your hips and your shoulders. If the gestures are higher, you will block your face. If they are lower, such as down around your thighs, they will be too far away from your face to be meaningful. When you think your message is going out to your audience, this is very easy to do.

To Build Voice Projection

Tape yourself during this exercise. Imagine your voice has to reach a point just a few inches in front of you and present for a minute at that projection level. Next, imagine your voice has to reach across the table or to a point about six feet away from you. Present at that projection level for a minute. Repeat the process with your voice having to reach the opposite end of the room. Notice any shift in physical feelings that you have. (You'll likely feel the energy in your body moving up to your chest area or to your head or out to the room.) Play the tape back and listen to all three levels. As a listener, you will probably prefer the second or third level of projection. To ensure that you are at that healthy level, go for the physical feeling you felt at that level. That will tell you you are projecting effectively.

To Feel More Comfortable With Gestures

Stand in front of a mirror and present for a few minutes, deliberately using your hands to reinforce or illustrate what you are saying. You may initially feel funny, but notice how much more animated and interesting you look when you use your hands. Gesture with them in front of you, between your hips and your shoulders. A side benefit is that the more you allow yourself your natural gestures, the more your voice picks up variety and increased intonation and you become even more interesting to listen to and watch.

To Strengthen Eye Contact

If you have trouble holding eye contact in group situations, practice at home, using pillows or pieces of paper with cartoon faces drawn on them taped to chairs. Place the pillows or cartoon faces around the room. Then, talk to each one for about the length of a sentence, a phrase, or until your voice folds down on your thought. It may seem very long to you, but in reality, it isn't. Get friends or family members to sit in as audience.

To Build Confidence

Videotape yourself. It's the best way to see how good you are naturally when you are delivering a presentation that has been carefully thought out, and when you are talking from the heart with conviction and enthusiasm!

- Be fair. Remember, you are your own worst critic.
- Practice. Speak up at meetings.
- Play charades with friends. Get used to being in front of people.
- Join your local Toastmasters International chapter.

13

"Smooth" Jazz

How to Handle Questions and Answers

"Look, I know I'm here to answer some tough questions,
but could I have some easy ones to warm up with?"

As sure as *re* follows *do* on the musical scale, you will have to answer two kinds of questions either during or after your presentation: simple ones and hard ones. Simple questions are the straightforward ones for which you have immediate answers. Hard questions are those that require more thought, are ambiguous, or are hostile. In all cases, your answers should strike the right chord in buyers, both in content and in tone of voice.

Strategy and skill rather than knee-jerk reactions work best and will give you the control you need in handling questions. First, however, you need to get questions.

Getting Questions When You Want Them

In formal presentations, set the procedure for questions during the introduction of your presentation. For example:

- *As we go through this, please ask questions at any point.*
- *Please note your questions. I will be happy to answer them at the end.*
- *Some of this information is fairly complex. People always have questions, so please feel free to ask questions at any time.*

If you are taking questions at the end of the presentation, step forward and open your hands slightly in an inviting way as you ask for questions. That encourages people to ask and it builds confidence in your buyers' minds that you are open to questions.

Instead of saying *Are there any questions?*, assume there are and ask, *What questions can I answer?* They will come more easily.

If you want questions while you're explaining really complex material and you're not getting them, say, *People always have questions about our methodology. Please, as we go through this chart, ask your questions.*

If you want questions at the end of your presentation and none are coming, give people an easy prompt like *Let me begin the question and answer session by . . .*, and follow it with a question. For example,

- *Let me begin the Q & A portion of our meeting today by answering a frequently asked question, which is . . .*
- *I noticed during the presentation that several of you seemed surprised at the results we were able to achieve. Let me begin the Q & A session by answering how it is we were able to do that. . . .*
- *People often ask me, how . . .? The answer is . . . What other questions do you have?*

If there are absolutely no questions forthcoming, assume the sale and say, *Great. When would you like to start?*

Managing Questions

Quick decisions need to be made when you are asked a question. Figure 13-1 provides a useful framework for making those decisions. Examples and an explanation of the nuances behind this decision model follow.

Handling questions requires good listening skills. When you get a question, listen for the issue and any emotion or ambiguity in the question. For example, *What is the price?*, when said in a genuine, inquiring tone of voice, is different from *So, what is the price?*, if spoken with a sarcastic snarl.

Your next decision is whether you want to answer the question yourself or open it up for group discussion. For example, someone asks, *What if we shortened the time frame on this project and tested only twenty stores rather than thirty?* To open this up for discussion, say, *How do the rest of you feel about this?* Or *What do the rest of you think?*

If you decide it's best to answer the question directly, do so. Your buyer asks, *What is the rate for all this?* You answer, *The rate is $. . .*

What if your buyer is clearly confused or misinformed? Resist a natural urge to say in an exasperated tone, *Well! as I said before . . .* It is never smart to make buyers look ignorant or foolish, particularly in a group. It is more diplomatic to use a helping phrase, such as, *Let me clarify that,* or affirm the buyer's question first, and then respond. Don't argue. For example:

Figure 13-1. Framework for making quick decisions.

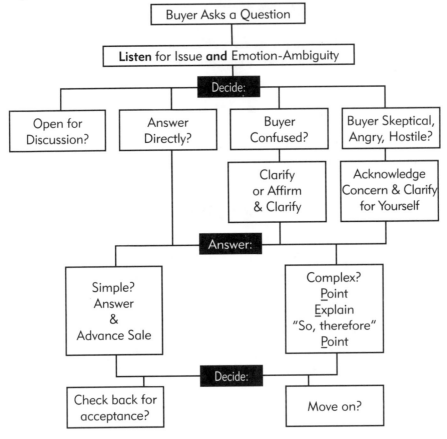

Question: *Why did my friend at Company X pay a lower rate for his group?*

Seller: *Let me clarify that.* He was here off-season, when rates are lower.

Or

Affirm & Clarify: *Yes, your rates seem higher. Actually, his group was here off-season, when rates are lower everywhere.*

Or

I can see why you might think your friend got a better deal. Actually, . . .

You're being agreeable without agreeing. There is a big difference between the two.

Smarter Answers to Simple Questions

Simple questions are usually requests for information. *When is the start date? Who will head the team? Who else have you done this for?*

You could just give the factual answer and you would satisfy your buyer. However, a Jazz! presenter will use the questions in Figure 13-1 with simple factual answers as opportunities to advance the sale. (See Figure 13-2.)

The key here is to give just a *little* more positive information and/or benefit to your buyer. Do not ramble or you will dilute the effect of your answer.

Difficult Questions

How do you handle the questions, and questioners, from hell? First, do not personalize the question. If this person is attacking

Figure 13-2. Answers for selling power.

Question	Simple Response	Jazz! Response
When is the start date?	June 1	*June 1*, which will get you finished in time for your fall product launch.
Who will head the team?	Rene Mason	*Rene Mason*, who has worked on twelve similar projects, so she is very familiar with the nuances of situations like yours.
Who else have you done this for?	ABC, XYZ, etc.	That's one of our strengths. *We have done this for ABC, XYZ, etc.*, the leading companies in your industry.

your arguments, it may mean you haven't made yourself clear, persuaded him, or neutralized all his fears or concerns about your Idea or Recommendation. If this person just has a difficult personality, then try to remember that, in the great scheme of things, he's got the bigger problem. Also, in a group setting, his colleagues are likely used to his histrionics and find him to be the same kind of nuisance you do.

To handle skeptical, angry, or hostile questions, acknowledge the person's feeling, clarify the issues that are prompting his negative feelings, and then respond. If you feel you need some time to think, then paraphrase, repeat, or invert the question.

- Question: (in a challenging tone of voice) *What do you offer at RMR for real daredevils?*

  Seller: (not wishing to walk into a trap, **clarifies** the question) *Interesting. Why do you ask?*

  Questioner: *Well, last time the only challenging activity for some of our wannabe sports nuts was hang gliding and three people got hurt. I want to make sure there is a variety of challenging, but safe, activities for these folks to enjoy.*

  Seller: (now clearer about the issue behind the challenge in the question, answers) *Not to worry! They can get their thrills white-water rafting and hiking—both exhilarating and much safer than hang gliding.*

- Question: (hostile tone) *Why don't you provide training in the cost of your system the way most other companies do?*

  Seller: (**paraphrase**) *With regard to training, we . . .*

- Question: (challenging tone) *How long will this take?*

  Seller: (**repeating**) *How long will this take? Depending on the resources you commit to this, it can take as little as . . .*

- Question: (skeptical tone, negative language) *Why should we believe you when your company screwed up so badly last time?*

  Seller: (Choosing *not* to repeat this, **paraphrases**) *The issue you're raising is, how can you be sure of success on this project?*

- Question: (skeptical tone) *How do I know this will work?*
  Seller: (**inverts**) *The reason you can be sure it will work is . . .*

Ambiguous Questions

If you decide the buyer's question is not hostile, but unclear or ambiguous, it's wise to clarify, or you might wind up answering the wrong question, or missing the real concern behind the question. For example,

> Question: *What about travel?*
> Seller: (not exactly sure what aspect of travel the buyer means, asks) *What specific question do you have about travel?*
> Questioner: *The travel time from each coast.*
> Seller: (still not 100 percent clear) *That can vary, depending on the airline. What exactly do you mean?*
> Questioner: *Well, we had a lot of complaints last year because people had to change planes more than once to get to the resort.*
> Seller: (now she fully understands and can answer) *I see. One of the best things about RMR is that most flights are direct from the major cities by most airlines, so people don't have to go through those tiring plane changes.*

PEP Up Answers to Hard Questions

Hard questions are those that require justification or greater explanation than questions with straightforward factual answers. Simple positive statements alone are not convincing responses. Use the PEP formula, which is like a minipresentation in itself, to answer these types of questions.

P   Make your **P**oint
E   **E**xplain, giving at least one **E**xample or supporting fact
       Add a conclusion phrase like *So,* or *So, therefore . . .*
P   Restate your **P**oint in similar words or spirit

Compare the Selling Power of These Answers

Question: *How can we be sure you'll finish on time?*
Seller: 1. *Because we always have.*
versus
2. **P**   *Because we always have.*
   E   *Our people are multitasked, so that they find and fix errors much more quickly than a team of specialists do. For example, at XYZ Company, our people realized problem X . . . within two days. The vice president told me that on a previous job, it took a week before his narrowly focused specialist team people figured out what was wrong,*
   So,
   P   *With this depth of experience, you can be assured that we will finish on time for you.*

Question: *Why is the price so high?*
Seller: 1. *Because we're so unique.*
versus
2. *With regard to our pricing,*
   P   *The value here is in the uniqueness of RMR.*
   E   *RMR has a combination of things to offer your people that you said you couldn't get at the other resort: activities, cuisine, facilities, and incredible views.*
   So, bottom line,
   P   *You will reap the rewards of this meeting many times over its cost.*

Question: *Can you guarantee that everyone will have a great time?*
Seller: 1. *Yes.*
versus
2. **P**   *There are no guarantees in life, Mr. Buyer, but RMR has everything going for it that is likely to give your folks a fabulous time.*
   E   *They can . . ., . . ., and . . . The facilities are . . . and the views are . . .*
   So,
   P   *It would be hard to find a place where the odds are better than they are at RMR for a great meeting.*

Question: *How does RMR compare to The Mountain Inn down the road?*
Seller: 1. *RMR offers more options.*
versus

2. **P** *RMR offers more options.*
   E *For example, RMR has eight tennis courts. They have only two. RMR has a spa. They don't. RMR has its own horses for riding. They don't.*
   Basically,
   P *You get much more for your money at RMR.*

Check Back or Move On?

Depending on the group, your time, the complexity of your product or service, and the appeal of the question to the rest of the group, you would decide either to check for acceptance of your answer or to move on. For example, if you decide to check back to ensure that the person understood your answer, you could say:

+ *Does that make sense?*
+ *Have I made that clearer for you?*
+ *Do you agree?*

Alternatively, you may just return to your presentation or take the next question. If you return to the presentation, do it in a smooth way. Don't just jerk your attention from the questioner to your material, as if to signal he was a bothersome interruption. Instead, *bridge* back from the questioner to your material. For example:

+ *Building on what you just asked, Mr. Buyer, when you look further at . . .* (and return to your material).
+ *What will be even more important to you, Mr. Buyer, than the . . . will be how we . . .* (and return to the next visual in your presentation).
+ *Your question leads us to the next point of interest for you. We can . . .* (and return to your presentation).

Right Question, Wrong Time

A common problem is being asked a question about something you will cover several pages later in the presentation. If you tell people to wait, they become annoyed. Worse, the unanswered question in their minds gets in the way of them hearing anything else you are saying. The best thing to do is to give a short answer and tell them:

1. You'll be coming to a fuller explanation shortly, or,
2. Explain why it's in their interest to wait for the fuller explanation.

For example,

Question: *How do you compare to competitor X in terms of your approach?*
Seller: *We'll be covering that in a few minutes, but the short answer is in our testing methodology. The reason for that will become clearer when you first understand the history behind the company and the kinds of work we've done with companies like yours.*

Then, move back to the presentation and continue.

Q & A and Your Eyes

During presentations, it is a good idea to look at people for about the length of a thought or phrase, as we discussed in Chapter 12. However, in handling questions, you play your eyes a little differently, depending on the situation.

In a large group, when someone asks a hard question, you know that it is a good idea to paraphrase, repeat, or invert the question. This gives you some time to think and it is a simple courtesy to the whole group to be sure everyone has heard the question. Take your eyes off the questioner and do this to the whole group.

Then, assume that everyone in the room wants the answer, and during the course of your answer, look at a few different people, including the person who asked the question. When you're done, you may glide your eyes to the next questioner, or you may return to the original questioner for a second and then glide your eyes elsewhere for the next question. If you linger on your questioner, chances are he or she will ask another question and suddenly you're locked into that person when you may not want to be.

If, however, you want to ensure that someone understood your answer, end your question with your eyes on the questioner for a couple of moments, looking for that understanding in his or her eyes. Then, glide your eyes to the next questioner or back to your material.

Warning: Always remember to use your judgment. If the person asking the question is the president of the company, you may well decide that it's politically smart to look at him throughout your answer and to check with your eyes, or with a spoken question (*Is that clearer now?*), to make sure he or she is satisfied with your answer.

Taking Questions Off-Line

For truly hostile questioners, or for people who seem to be the only ones not understanding the presentation, acknowledge them and say you'll take their questions off-line during the break. For example:

- *It's clear you feel strongly about this. Let's meet on the break and talk further then. Right now, in the interest of time, we need to move on.*
- *I'd be happy to go over the numbers with you during the break. However, we need to move on so that everyone can ask their questions.*

(Move your eyes immediately to the next questioner or back to your presentation).

When You Don't Know the Answer

When you don't know the answer, say so. Don't lie. *I'm sorry I don't have that information. I will be happy to get it to you by this afternoon.*

Then move immediately to the next questioner or back to the presentation.

When Q & A Is Over

Finally, when the Q & A period is over, return to your summary. People remember the last thing they hear. If you just say thank you, they will remember the answer to the last question, which is what you most likely do not want. Make it short, but get the summary in before people leave.

If there are no more questions, let's quickly recap.

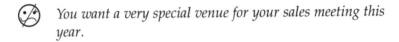

You want a very special venue for your sales meeting this year.

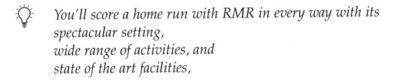

You'll score a home run with RMR in every way with its spectacular setting,
wide range of activities, and
state of the art facilities,

All of which will give you an unforgettable meeting.

A letter of intent and a deposit today will hold your August dates for you.

Clinkers

There are two major clinkers to avoid. First, keep your answers short. Avoid rambling. If you feel yourself going on and on, simply say, *So, therefore . . .*, which generally brings you back to your point and lets you end the answer.

The second clinker is the poorly timed use of the phrase *I think . . .* by the seller. This usually happens when you are challenged and the buyer says, for example, *I don't think your proposal has enough contingencies in it for any downturn in the economy* and you respond, *Oh, I think it does because . . .* Your *I think it does* is like waving a red flag in front of a snorting bull. Your buyer will only dig his heels in deeper and attack you. *Well, I think it doesn't!* This is often followed by a heated attack on your credentials and/or your experience, which tends to make you become tense, defensive, and adversarial. Nothing good can come from this exchange.

Watch your pronouns. A better response would be to clarify why your buyer feels that way. Then, before you answer, acknowledge or affirm his view and stick to the issues/facts in your answer. Do not personalize the answer.

> Seller: *You say the proposal lacks contingencies for an unexpected downturn. Can you tell me which contingencies you mean? (Or, What leads you to conclude that? Or, Why do you feel that way?)*
>
> Questioner: *Your proposal assumes a 7 percent increase in revenues from our current customers. I've been in this business a long time and I think that is a very unrealistic number. If we get a downturn, we'll never get more than 4 to 5 percent. Then what will happen!*
>
> Seller: (affirm & stick with the issues or facts) *We looked very carefully at the projected revenue. In fact, the 7 percent projection is a very conservative number. The research with your best customers indicates an 11 percent increase if the economy remains strong and a 9 to 10 percent increase if there is a downturn. So, a 7 percent figure is more than a reasonable assumption.*

At that point, depending on who the questioner is, you can ask if that is clearer now, or you can move your eyes to the next questioner, or return to your presentation if his question was an interruption.

In the Spotlight: Your Turn

Think about how you handle questions both in one-to-one presentations and in more formal group situations. Write down three factual questions that you tend to get from buyers. Write down three challenging or complex questions you also tend to get. Using the ideas, tips, and strategies in this chapter, how would you now answer them? Tape yourself, if possible.

1. For each factual question, advance your cause and add an additional benefit or a brief piece of additional information. Factual Question:

   Answer (Advance the Cause):

2. For each difficult question, paraphrase, invert, or repeat it. Then respond, using the **PEP** formula. Difficult Question:

   (Paraphrase, invert, repeat?):

   (Respond):

   Point:

   Explain:

   Point:

Use the grid in Figure 13-3 to check how you tend to answer questions. Practice the techniques in this chapter to help you handle this part of a presentation as smoothly as possible.

Summary

1. Handling questions is an integral part of a presentation.
2. Listen carefully to questions for both the issues they raise

Figure 13-3. Are you in control of Q & A?

Novice	Are You in Control of Q & A Average	Star
Gives knee-jerk answers	Often misses the emotion/ambiguity	Listens for issue and emotion/ambiguity
	Sometimes becomes defensive or adversarial with answers	Processes questions Rarely becomes defensive or adversarial
Handles difficult questions poorly	Sometimes handles difficult questions poorly	Consistently handles difficult questions well
	Uses simple questions to sell additional benefits	Uses simple questions to sell additional benefits
	Sometimes uses PEP	Uses PEP regularly
Jumps from questioner back to presentation	Sometimes bridges from questioner to presentation	Bridges from questioner to presentation
Rarely summarizes after Q & A	Sometimes summarizes after Q & A	Regularly summarizes after Q & A
Often appears out of control	Sometimes appears confident and in control	Always appears confident and in control

and for the tone and feeling behind them. Then respond strategically.

3. Let answers to questions become part of the rhythm of your presentation in a professional and upbeat way and contribute to its overall selling power.

Conclusion

Play the Mu$ic That Keeps on Selling

If this book has an underlying belief, it is that every salesperson can be a star presenter. There is no mystery behind creating and giving a winning sales presentation. There are some things to know and a willingness to practice them. But there are no secrets privy only to select salespeople (and presentation skills book writers).

In an article for *The New York Times*, renowned pianist and New England Conservatory teacher Russell Sherman observed, "Catching a sound, like catching a fish, is a function not of physical prowess but of the hand's sensitivity in gauging the currents and resistance of the musical flow."*

Likewise, a winning presentation is not a function of some heroic power but of your sensitivity as a salesperson in gauging the currents and resistance of the flow of elements that comprise any presentation.

Those elements are the basic principles of human learning and psychology that you've seen demonstrated in the Jazz! framework. Jazz! integrates those principles into an easy to use, efficient, reliable, and repeatable framework so that they come together to give the fullest expression and selling power to your message.

Like a sheet of music, the more you play these elements, or notes, the easier they are to repeat. Also, like playing music, the

*Russell Sherman, "Ah, to Have Chopin's Hands or Even Rubinstein's Pinkies," *The New York Times*, June 26, 1994. Copyright © 1994 by The New York Times Co. Reprinted by permission.

better you know the notes and the melody, the more creative you will become with them.

What are these principles? They're composites of the lists you saw in the introduction to this book, when I asked you to write down how you felt when you saw a strong presentation.

The first principle is that **people like order.** They like their presentations to have a clear beginning, middle, and end with easy-to-follow transitions in between. The Jazz! framework satisfies that need.

A second principle is that **people like to feel important and cared about.** When your introduction is buyer-focused, the buyer feels good. When you use buyer-centered pronouns, instead of "I" pronouns, the buyer feels important. When you highlight the benefits of your information to his or her world, the buyer feels cared about. When your summary is buyer-focused, the buyer feels cared about, important, and good. Jazz! keeps the focus where it belongs: on your buyer.

A third principle is that **people don't like to have their time wasted.** When you focus on your Buyer's Objective and Situation in your introduction, the buyer sees value in giving you his attention. When you relate your information to benefits or conclusions meaningful to the buyer, the buyer continues to pay attention. When you reinforce the value of your ideas to his objectives in your summary, the buyer is still paying attention. To a buyer, *his* world is never a waste of time to him. The Jazz! framework makes good use of everyone's time in a presentation.

People don't like to be bored. When you provide helpful examples and stories, your presentation is interesting. When you use analogies, your presentation is not only interesting but dramatic and memorable as well. When you translate cold, abstract numbers into something concrete and familiar to the buyer, your presentation is interesting. When you use relevant quotations and testimonials, your presentation is interesting. When you show lively visuals that are easy to read and look at, your presentation is interesting, and, where appropriate, fun. When you involve buyers in the presentation, your presentation is interesting and also more fun. When you add appropriate creative touches, your presentation is even more compelling and interesting.

Using the Jazz! icons (or Avery dots) to check how your information is being presented will tell you how interesting your presentation is. There may be many reasons for losing a piece of business, but there is *no* excuse for losing that business because the buyer was bored by your presentation.

Another principle is that **people respond to positive energy.** When buyers sense a genuine desire on your part to help them, they feel positive toward you. They also feel positive toward you when they see your conviction, passion, and belief in your product or service in your eyes, voice, and body movements.

A huge bonus of using the Jazz! framework is that it naturally enhances your delivery skills. It's similar to what happens when you put a suit on someone who slouches. No matter how beautiful the external suit, it doesn't look particularly good if the structure under it is drooping. As soon as the person stands up straight and proud, that suit will look better because the underlying structure is sound. The same holds true with your delivery skills. A sound presentation structure containing the elements that recognize basic human learning and psychology principles will always strengthen your personal delivery skills. Conversely, the best delivery skills in the world won't compensate for a presentation that fails to recognize these principles. You may be very entertaining and you may even fool a few buyers from time to time, but in the long term, style without substance is a loser's strategy. Jazz! provides the substance that allows you to look stylish.

The Future

No one can tell exactly what the future brings, but one can place some reasonable bets. One bet is that constant technological change, a continually accelerating sales pace, widening globalization, and tougher competition are likely to continue into the future. Another is that whether the interface between buyer and seller is across a table, over a computer, or via a videoconference, salespeople will still have to present the value of their products or services to customers.

Winning will go to the disciplined, to the creative, and to those professionals who constantly aim to be among the stars in their field. Jazz! is the instrument that can help you be one of those stars, a salesperson whose presentations *move* people to make a commitment, to say yes!

Appendix A

What Do I Do If . . .?

Preparation

How Long Should a Presentation Be?

My answer is the same one my English teacher gave us in high school when we asked how long an assigned book report had to be. Mrs. Harris would respond, "A book report is like a woman's skirt. It should be long enough to cover the subject and short enough to keep it interesting!" A good way to test the effectiveness of the length of your presentation is to practice it in front of a colleague.

Should I Script My Presentations in Advance?

Some people prefer to write out an entire script, go over it a few times to get comfortable with the concepts, and then reduce the script to notes. Others like to note just the key points, examples, stories, and analogies for each piece of information, and then weave it together in real time with the client.

Either alternative works. What doesn't work is to memorize the presentation. If you forget a word, you'll get stuck. And, unless you are a very good actor, you will ultimately sound canned.

How Do I Ensure Successful Team Presentations?

Use the Jazz! system to think through and prepare the presentation. If someone else is going to do the actual visuals, get that person in on your planning process immediately. Rehearse very thoroughly several times. Get agreement with team members on the objective of the meeting and on the desired action step. Also get agreement on who the team leader is in case unexpected decisions need to be made, such as the buyer cutting your time by half. Have someone proofread the visuals very carefully. There's nothing like a typographical error to undermine your credibility. Assign roles. Will one person do the introductions, or will each team member introduce himself or herself? Who will take which parts of the presentation? How will you pass the baton to the next speaker? Who will answer which questions? How will you gracefully interrupt each other? (For example, *Let me build on what Harry is saying . . .* or, *Marge, if I may, here's another point that will be of interest to the group . . .*) Who will summarize?

During the presentation, when a team member is speaking, the others should be splitting their attention between what that person is saying and the reactions of the buyers in the room. Team members should not be doodling, looking at their notes, or staring at the ceiling.

When it's time for you to present your part of the presentation, use a modified version of the Jazz! introduction. You wouldn't necessarily show anything in these remarks. The few seconds it takes to make these remarks give people a chance to make the adjustment to you and your voice and for both you and your buyer to get on the same beat.

For example, suppose your colleague Paula finishes explaining your company's credentials and past experience and says, *Next, Pat will explain how we would tailor this project to your needs.* As Pat, you would say:

> *As you've seen, XYZ Company has done a lot of work in your industry.*
>
> **?** *Now, how would we work with you?*
>
> *Basically, it's a disciplined approach that begins with interviews with key staff members and goes through to post-implementation follow-up and measurement.*

☺   *The whole process is designed to give you the results you want.*

❯   *Let's start with the interviews . . .*

Debrief after a team presentation. What worked? What didn't? What do we want to do differently in future team presentations?

How Do I Keep Long, Technical Presentations Interesting?

Use the Jazz! system to organize your presentation. Have an agenda so people can see where you are taking them. If there are several sections to your presentation, you can have a word in shadow at the top or in a lower corner of each visual that indicates where you are on the agenda. Make the visuals colorful. Make sure there is variety to the types of visuals.

Use examples and analogies to help people understand your material more easily and to keep it interesting.

Periodically, do minisummaries so that you make it easy for buyers to stay in your story. Have some points in the presentation where you can involve the group. Throw the floor open for discussion; ask for questions.

Why Do I Have to Use So Much Repetition: Repeating Key Buyer Points, Using Minisummaries, Repeating My Idea/Recommendation at the End?

People need to hear things many times before a new idea really sinks in. Just think of your own experience learning a second language in school. First, you heard the new word. Then, you said the word several times. Next, you used it in a sentence, and last, you practiced it many times over, until it became part of your vocabulary.

The same is true in a presentation. Your buyer hears your Idea/Recommendation in the introduction for the first time. She hears it proved and reinforced in the middle of the presentation several times before it imprints itself in her mind again when she hears it in the summary. The same is true with Key Buyer Points. Repetition burns them into your buyer's consciousness.

Corporations understand this power of repetition. They spend millions of dollars running the same advertisement many times in publications and on television. They know that a single impression in your mind, even a good impression, is not likely to stick. The image needs to be reinforced several times for it to lock into your consciousness.

Does the Jazz! Framework Apply When I'm Not Selling Anything in My Presentation but Just Informing My Buyers About Something?

If you are just informing your buyer about something simple and factual, like a change in the list of service contacts at your company, then you would not need the Jazz! framework. However, if you are informing a buyer about your general capabilities, then you would use the Jazz! framework. What objective of theirs is satisfied by knowing this information? What's their situation that makes them need this information? You will still talk about the benefits of your capabilities, give examples, use analogies, tell stories, and involve them. You will still use transitions for a smooth flow. You will still summarize. The Action Step may not be an order, but it could be the right to bid on an upcoming project of theirs.

Specific Skills and Logistics

How Can I Improve My Vocabulary to Make My Descriptions and Claims More Interesting and Vivid for My Buyers?

Buy a thesaurus, which is a dictionary of synonyms. For example, if you want to say that your product is special, but *special* is an overused adjective, a quick check in the thesaurus will provide alternative descriptions, such as *remarkable, striking, distinguished, exceptional, unique, extraordinary, offbeat, unusual, phenomenal, unprecedented, singular, rare, amazing, breathtaking,* and *wonderful.*

Clip and save interesting stories, quotes, cartoons, and analogies that you come across in your normal newspaper and magazine reading.

Aim to sprinkle a new word into your conversations each day or week. Buy a vocabulary improvement book at your local bookstore.

Listen to good speakers.

Read well-written publications like *Outside Magazine, Sports Illustrated, The New Yorker, The Atlantic Monthly,* and *Smithsonian.*

Is It Better to Sit or Stand?

Always stand in either small or large groups. You have more control and can see reactions. You appear more authoritative. It's easier to hold attention. Some salespeople even choose to stand during a one-on-one presentation. Studies at 3M and the Wharton School of Business showed that people who stood and presented with visuals were perceived as more credible and persuasive.

Is It Necessary to Move Around?

Some people are quite effective moving. Others are equally effective staying more or less in one spot, although allowing movement in the hands to reinforce points. What's important is that you do what is effective. If you do move, make it purposeful. Move toward the buyer to make a point. Move to the screen to make a point. Don't just pace back and forth looking at the floor.

What Should I Do With My Hands During a Seated Presentation?

Keep them comfortably on the table, available to you for gestures just as in a stand-up presentation. Keep the gestures between the table and your shoulders, so you don't block your face. Avoid sitting with crossed arms; you will look hostile, tense up, and eventually drop into a monotone.

Is It Wrong to Hold Onto a Pen When I'm Standing? It Makes Me More Comfortable.

You can do anything as long as it doesn't distract from your presentation. Many people like to hold onto a pen to be comfortable. If you don't play with it, if you don't use it to point at your audience, if it doesn't get in the way of normal gestures, then you can hold onto it.

Is It All Right to Hold Onto My Notes?

It is better not to do that. That is likely to become really awkward. Put your notes beside the projector. No one minds if you glance down at them occasionally for your next thought.

Strategy

How Do I Defuse Negative Viewpoints or Hidden Agendas?

Make a pre-emptive strike! You can do this in any of three places in your presentation. In the Buyer's Situation, step in the introduction:

The situation is . . . *And also, there are many different views in the room as to the best way to solve the problem.*

So, the question is, how can we help?

We recommend . . .

Your acknowledgement of their different views makes people feel recognized. They will usually give you the benefit of the doubt and allow you to present with less interruption.

Another defusion point is at the end of the introduction:

As a result, this will help meet your objectives. *As we go into further detail, what you'll see is controversial and you'll have questions and, perhaps, some strong reactions. Let me suggest that we go through the facts first and then we can have an open discussion of the issues at the end.*

> Let's begin with . . .

A third spot is at the beginning of some information and/or visual that will arouse controversy.

These next few visuals about our approach may raise some controversial points. Please ask your questions or voice your concerns as we review this material.

How Do I Deal With Competition in the Presentation?

Never knock the competition. However, you can show quantitative comparisons using graphs and charts. You can discuss true success stories with your other clients. You can establish buying criteria in your buyer's mind that favor your product or service. For example:

All information centers are not the same. It becomes critical that you have X kind of information and that you have it set up in the right way or else you risk wiping out two years' work in one month. We have seen this happen time and again. For example, . . .

When the competition presents after you, you can bet the first question from the buyer will be, *What kind of information does your center have and how is it set up?*

Another way to enhance your competitive credibility is to pepper your presentation with references to well-known industry journals, books, leaders, speakers, recent events, sayings, or conferences. Your buyers will have more confidence in you when they see that you really do know their industry.

On October 27, 1997, when the stock market plummeted more than 554 points, I had the dubious task of running a previously scheduled evening presentation skills miniworkshop for a group of securities traders, whom I had not met before, at a leading investment banking firm. After that wild trading day, it was no surprise that next to learning how to strengthen their presentation skills, meeting me was the last thing they wanted to do that evening.

Early in my opening remarks, which acknowledged the amazing day they had just experienced, I made sure to mention that I had worked on a trading desk at one point, had sold advertising space for *Institutional Investor* magazine (a publication they knew well), and that I had actually run a similar seminar for a group of investment bankers the day the market crashed in 1987. I then added what they also already knew, that about five months after that crash, the market took off for one of the longest bull markets in history.

My strategic name- and fact-dropping notwithstanding, I'm sure those traders still would have preferred to go home, but at least I could see them relax with me personally. Happily, they soon relaxed into the seminar as well.

How Do I Emphasize Certain Information or Key Buyer Points?

Use language spotlights. These are phrases such as *The really important point to note here is . . . The key number is . . . If you remember nothing else, remember . . . What's particularly critical is . . . The absolutely essential factor for this to succeed will be . . .*

How Can I Create a Sense of Urgency?

Gently suggest that it is in the client's best interest to act now rather than later. For example:

> Of course, you could delay setting up an information center, and, indeed, that is the right action for some number of companies. *However, experience shows that if your assessment is inaccurate, you could lose . . . over the next two years.*

Should I Tell Jokes?

Generally, it is a bad idea to tell jokes. However, it is a good idea to let your spontaneous, natural sense of humor come through during the presentation. If you are tempted to use a joke, it should make a point related to the presentation. No matter how funny, avoid religious, political, gender, race, ethnic, or double-entendre jokes. You never know who has what sensibilities, or who is married to whom, or who has what background. However, if you are determined to tell a joke, be sure to test it *carefully* with colleagues first.

What if I Sense I Am Losing My Client?

First, check your energy level. If it has dropped, your listeners have similarly dropped their attention. Raise it on your next thought. If that doesn't revive their interest, stop. Get them involved. Ask for a reaction or response. Be honest and simply ask if you are talking about what they want to hear.

How Do I Deal With Irrelevant Questions?

Acknowledge them. Take them off-line. Move on to the next questioner or return to the next point in the presentation.

> *That is an interesting point, Dan. I'd be happy to review the numbers with you in greater detail over lunch. However, in the interest of time, we need to move on. (Move gracefully to the next questioner.) Yes, Jack, you had a question?*

What if I Am Much Younger or Older Than My Buyers?

If you can legitimately solve their problems or add value to their business situation, and if you "know your stuff" and dress and behave professionally, it doesn't matter how old or young you are. However, you would be foolish to do anything that drew attention to that age gap. If you're young, avoid peppering your presentation with phrases like *you guys*, or using *okay* when you've finished making a point. Find another adjective besides *awesome* to describe the extraordinary performance of your product. Also, buyers really don't have to hear *you know* between phrases. Avoid the word *like* as in *Like, first we do . . . which is, like, really powerful because, like . . .* If you don't avoid these words and phrases, then, *like, it's really hard for older people to, you know, take you seriously.*

Conversely, if you are older, references are lost on your buyers when you refer to the war and you mean World War II. With some buyers today, even the Vietnam War is something that happened a long time ago, beyond their memory. I had this brought home to me several years ago when I asked a group to remember where they were when John F. Kennedy was shot. Not one person raised his hand. Momentarily stunned that these people didn't remember the defining moment of my generation because they weren't born yet, I quickly regrouped and asked them to recall where they were when the space shuttle *Challenger* blew up. That tragedy occurred about twelve years ago; mercifully, so far none of my buyers have ever been so young that they don't remember that.

Visual Aids

Should I Give Out a Copy of the Presentation?

Not usually. People will jump ahead of you. It is better to tell your audience there will be a copy for everyone afterward. Alternatively, you can distribute handouts during the presentation when you come to those specific visuals in the presentation.

How Long Do I Stay On a Visual?

As little as thirty seconds, depending on the content. In a highly technical presentation, you would need to spend more time than on one that is relatively easy to understand.

What Visuals Are Essential?

Generally speaking, visuals are necessary for a title page, which should have the client's name or logo on it; your Idea or Recommendation; the supporting information; the summary of your Idea or Recommendation; and the Action Steps.

Optional visuals, depending on the complexity and the situation, would be of the client's situation and the agenda.

Do I Need to Have a Visual for Every Information Point?

No. However, if you are going to talk through a point without a visual, shut off the projector or move to a blank in your computer. Attention will be drawn to you, which is where it should be. If you're working with an overhead projector, when you are ready to continue with the next visual, put the next transparency on the machine first, then turn the light on and continue, or with your computer, click to the next visual and continue.

Can I Use More Than One Medium?

Absolutely. If you are using transparencies or even an electronic presentation with ten to twenty people, you can break and go to a flip chart and easel to work through a live problem with the group. Often that spontaneous portion of your presentation will sell you more than all the bells and whistles in your prepared presentation.

What Can I Do if My Transparencies Are Only Black and White?

If you are working with transparencies, have red, green, and blue markers with you. Use them periodically during the presentation to circle a number, underline a point, draw an arrow on a graph, or trace a path through a complex process. Another idea is to get colored transparencies and run your report out on them. For important presentations, the best idea is to avoid black and white transparencies.

Should I Dim the Lights for a Slide or Electronic Presentation?

Dim is okay. Dark is not. People will go to sleep and, at the very least, you will lose the chance to make eye contact.

Is It Okay to Have Notes?

Yes, but use them discreetly. Don't hold them in your hand. If you are using transparencies, then you can have big notes in red ink on the hard copy next to the projector. If you are speaking from behind a lectern, big index cards or standard size pages are possible. However, do not write a script because you will wind up reading it. It is better to have a picture of your visual and two or three bullets next to it to remind you of what you want to say. The exception is if you have to quote someone or state something that legally must come out exactly a certain way.

If you are working with flip charts, you can draw in light pencil a key word or the visual of the upcoming page. When you finish the page you are on, you simply look at the pencil note to remind you of what's coming next.

If you are using flip frames on overhead transparencies, there is enough room on the floppy side panels for notes. Be sure to keep the notes to key words or pictures. If you write out full sentences, you will start to "read" your notes and look very unprofessional.

What If I Drop My Overheads?

Always number your overheads on the frames, so you can re-order them quickly if they drop.

What's the Most Important Thing to Do for Any Presentation?

The answer is the same as it is in any professional activity, whether it's running a marathon, litigating a case in court, performing on stage, or presiding over a shareholders' meeting. Plan, practice, be positive, and give it your unconditional best shot!

Appendix B

Jazz! Formats and Summary

1. Review Figure 1-5. A Jazz! Introduction.
2.

A Jazz! Middle	
"Cook" With Your Buyers	
📁 Information	
❗ Key Buyer Points	Benefits
	Conclusions
💭 Word Pictures	Examples
	Stories
💭	Comparisons
	Abstract numbers made concrete
💭	Testimonials
	Quotations
↻ Involvement	You, Your pronouns
	Personalizing
	Mental
	Actual
＞ Transitions	Between Points
	Minisummaries

3. Review Figure 5-6. A Jazz! Summary.
4. Le Jazz Hot! The Creative Touch
   Use:
   • Appropriate stories
   • Startling facts
   • Quotations

- Provocative questions
- Props
- Games
- Analogies
- A theme that runs throughout the presentation
- Cartoons

5. *See* the Music: Visual Aids
   Use visuals: To illustrate, support, reinforce a point.
   Make visuals: Big, simple, clear, colorful.
   Best visuals: Bullets, graphs, charts, pictures.

6. Compose the (Sales) Music: Planning

CRITICAL QUESTIONS TO ANSWER

1. What is my objective?
2. How do I want buyers to feel at the end?
3. What is the most appropriate action step?
4. Who is my buyer?
5. What style(s) is he?
6. How sophisticated is the buyer about my product or service?
7. What is the appropriate tone for this meeting?
8. How much time will I have?
9. What is my Buyer's Objective and Situation?
10. What is My Idea or Recommendation?
    Best Story?
    Most effective vivid language?
11. What are my Key Buyer Points for this buyer?
    What information do I need to support each?
    What are the best visuals for these points?
    What Word Pictures do I need for interest and ease of under-
    standing?
    Where can I involve my buyer?
12. How can I be creative?
13. What questions will my buyer have?
    How will I address these?
    What should the procedure for questions be?
14. Who else should be on the call with me?

PRACTICE CHECKLIST

    1. Is the presentation buyer-focused?
    2. Is there a clear story with vivid language?
    3. Is the supporting information sequenced properly?
    4. Does the information effectively counter objections?
    5. Are there enough Word Pictures to help the buyer understand the information better?
    6. Are the Key Buyer Points clear?
    7. Does it flow? Are there effective Transitions and minisummaries?
    8. Is the tone right?
    9. Is it stylistically right for this buyer?
    10. Are the visuals clear, lively, and compelling?
    11. Have I built in opportunities to involve the buyer?
    12. Is the presentation appropriately creative?
    13. Is there a strong summary that makes it easy for this buyer to justify saying yes?

7. Smooth Jazz! Question-and-Answer Strategy
   Review Figure 13-1.

8. Play It Cool! Handling Group Presentation Jitters
   a. Prepare
      • Recall Jazz! symbols to cue thoughts in impromptu situations
      • Use Jazz! Formats for more formal presentations
   b. Practice five or six times
   c. Practice responses to expected hard questions
   d. Use positive self-talk to psyche yourself up
      • See yourself being successful
      • Review your opening several times
      • Breathe deeply to calm down
      • Hum to warm the vocal cords
      • Yawn to release tension
      • Use conversational, one-to-one eye contact
      • Stay focused in the moment *with* your buyers
      • Be enthusiastic and upbeat
      • *Have fun!*

Bibliography

Anderson, James. *Speaking to Groups*. Vienna, Va.: Wyndmoor Press, 1989.

Hoff, Ron. *I Can See You Naked*. Kansas City, Mo.: Andrews and McMeel, 1988.

Hughes, Langston. *The First Book of Jazz*. Hopewell, N.J.: Ecco Press, 1995.

Jordan, Michael. *I Can't Accept Not Trying*. San Francisco: Harper-Collins, 1994.

McBride, Dennis. *How to Make Visual Presentations*. New York: Art-Direction Book Company, 1982.

Nelson, Noelle C. *Winning! Using Lawyers' Courtroom Techniques to Get Your Way in Everyday Situations*. New York: Prentice-Hall Direct, 1997.

Peoples, David A. *Presentations Plus*. 2d ed. New York: John Wiley & Sons, 1992.

Raines, Claire. *Visual Aids in Business*. Los Altos, Calif.: Crisp Publications, 1989.

Strumpf, Stephen and Joel DeLuca. *Learning to Use What You Already Know*. San Francisco: Berrett-Kochler Publishers, 1994.

Trout, Jack and Al Ries. *Positioning: The Battle for Your Mind*. New York: Warner Books, 1993.

Trout, Jack, with Steve Rivkin. *The New Positioning*. New York: McGraw-Hill, 1996.

Tufte, John. *The Visual Display of Quantitative Information*. Cheshire, Conn.: Graphics Press, 1992.

Woodall, Marian. *Thinking on Your Feet*. Lake Oswego, Oreg.: Professional Business Communications, 1987.

Author Information

To share your comments, or, for further information on Anne Miller's sales and communications speeches, seminars, and audio-tapes, call 212-876-1875 or e-mail: amspeak@aol.com. Or you can write:

Anne Miller
Chiron Associates, Inc.
Box 624
New York, NY 10163

Index